Heart's Cry

Revised Edition

Heart's Cry

Principles of Prayer

Revised Edition

Jennifer Kennedy Dean

Birmingham, Alabama

New Hope® Publishers
P. O. Box 12065
Birmingham, AL 35202-2065
www.newhopepublishers.com

Library of Congress Cataloging-in-Publication Data

Dean, Jennifer Kennedy.
  Heart's cry : principles of prayer / Jennifer Kennedy Dean. -- Rev. ed.
    p. cm.
  Includes bibliographical references.
  ISBN 978-1-59669-095-0 (sc)
  1. Prayer. I. Title.
  BV220.D43 2007.
  248.3'2--dc22

                          2006033975

Cover design by The DesignWorks Group, Inc.
www.thedesignworksgroup.com

ISBN-10: 1-59669-095-X
ISBN-13: 978-1-59669-095-0
N074143 • 0207 • 7M1

Oh, Lord, who can stand when You appear?
The splendor of Your presence near
Then knee must bow and tongue proclaim
The pow'r of Your majestic name.

My hungry heart cries out for You.
No earthly substitute will do.
Refiner's Fire, come near to me
Your unveiled glory, let me see.

A heart like Yours, my one desire.
Do Your work, Refiner's Fire.

Your holy Fire now burns within
And purges every secret sin.
My life the bush, Your Life the Flame
That leaves me nevermore the same.

Your Life in me ignites the Fire
That now fulfills my heart's desire.
The Spirit's work, my life made new,
Transformed within, ablaze with You.

A heart like Yours, my one desire.
Do Your work, Refiner's Fire.

Dedication

In loving memory of my husband

Wayne Dean

How we miss his presence with us. Silly jokes, loud laugh, eyes
that twinkle in amusement, a little bossing, lots of opinions,
boundless generosity. Our lives are richer for having had him in
them.

"If ever two were one, then surely we;
If ever man were loved by wife, then thee."

(From *To My Dear and Loving Husband* by Anne Bradstreet)

Table of Contents

Foreword

Prayer. Is it a mystery to you? At times prayer is the most blessed thing I have in my life, and at other times I sit in wonder of how prayer actually works and why God chose to use that vessel to communicate with me. *Heart's Cry* is the one book that will unpack the word *prayer* and give it meaning and significance to your soul. Whether you are just now taking baby steps to communicating with your heavenly Father or whether you are a seasoned prayer warrior, there are words in *Heart's Cry* that will train and guide your conversation in the relationship that is critical to your spiritual walk. God could have chosen to sit in heaven and just look at our lives and "toss out" the answers we need, but that would not have satisfied His need for fellowship with us—the apple of His eye. Prayer becomes the conduit between the need and the provision God made to meet that need. So many Christians today walk around without a good grasp on the power of prayer—both individual and corporate. Jennifer Kennedy Dean has captured the basic principles of prayer and put them in a concise, easy-to-understand format. Is there a formula that will move the hand of God to answer our prayers? No. Prayer has never been about a formula—it's always been about the relationship. Sit back and read proven steps to guide you into a deeper intimacy with God and the result will be powerful and effective prayers (James 5:16).

Jim Weidmann, Vice-Chairman
National Day of Prayer Task Force

Introduction

I first wrote *Heart's Cry* 15 years ago. It was my very first book. To come back 15 years later to update it and get it ready to send back out again has been an interesting experience for me. Most interesting is that the things that God had taught me about prayer all those years ago are the things He is still teaching me.

I didn't change much in the book. I updated the illustrations, polished sentences, and spruced it up some. When I first wrote it, I thought I'd written all there was to say. Nearly every principle in the book I have written more extensively about in other books and studies. There is no end to the learning.

I recently experienced the unexpected illness and death of my husband, Wayne. He had an aggressive and advanced brain cancer. Two months after his diagnosis, the Lord took him home. As I write this, I am coming up on the first anniversary of those events that drastically changed the trajectory of my life. I am still reeling from the upheaval, and I am still at the mercy of the grief that sometimes overwhelms me. These times have presented me with the opportunity to let God prove His truth. I found myself using the things I have just experienced as illustrations of the very principles I wrote about 15 years ago.

When I wrote this book the first time, my children were young and under foot. Now my three sons are grown and gone from home. The same truths still stand, proven now more times than I can count.

Circumstances change. People change. Your environment changes. God remains the same.

If you are new to Bible study, I have added some explanatory notes where you might need more detail. Also, at the back of the book, you will find a list of resources that will help you grow and learn more about prayer, a teaching guide to help you share this book with others, and additional tools to help you get the most out of this book.

The Scripture tells us to encourage one another.

"Encourage one another and build each other up" (1 Thessalonians 5:11).

"Let us not give up meeting together, as some are in the habit of doing, but let us encourage one another—and all the more as you see the Day approaching" (Hebrews 10:25).

"May our Lord Jesus Christ himself and God our Father, who loved us and by his grace gave us eternal encouragement and good hope, encourage your hearts and strengthen you in every good deed and word" (2 Thessalonians 2:16–17).

In a recent newsletter, I asked people to send me stories and words of encouragement that would build up the body of Christ and encourage others in prayer. I asked especially for experiences in prayer groups. I'm going to let some of them tell you their stories in their own words. Here you will find encouragement, new ideas, and hope. That's what the body of Christ is all about—building one another up in the Lord. You'll find these stories scattered throughout the book in insets.

Do you have some words of encouragement to share? Go to www.hearts-cry.net and add your thoughts to the Wall of Encouragement.

Whether you are a seasoned pray-er or just beginning, consider finding a friend or a group to study this book with you. You can encourage each other, and you can have someone to discuss the concepts with, which usually stirs up your creativity and expands your thinking. At the back, there is a teaching guide to use with a group. It will work well as a private devotional study, though, if that is how you want to use it.

Look up all the Scriptures. Don't take my word for anything. Let this be an experience, not just a study.

May the Lord Himself teach you to pray.

If You Are New to Bible Study

If you are new to Bible study, you might feel overwhelmed by the number of Scripture references throughout this book. But, of course, the only textbook on prayer is the Bible, so it is crucial to know what the Bible has to say. There is no other authority. You will quickly learn to look up Scripture references, and it will be well worth your effort.

The Bible is divided into the Old Testament and the New Testament. In the front of your Bible, you will probably find an index of the books of the Bible, divided into Old and New Testaments. Some Bibles list the books alphabetically, and some list them in the order they occur.

Each book of the Bible is divided into chapters, and each chapter is divided into verses.

A Scripture reference such as John 3:16 refers to the Book of John, the third chapter, and the 16th verse in that chapter. John (book of the Bible) 3 (chapter in John): 16 (verse in that chapter).

The Old Testament was written before the birth of Jesus, and the New Testament begins with the birth of Jesus.

Each book of the Bible was written by a different author, although some authors wrote multiple books. The books of the Bible were written at different times in history and under different circumstances. Some of the books are written as recorded history, others are poetry, others a prophecy and warning, some are letters. Though the authors and the times and the circumstances differed, the whole Bible was inspired by God, and there is an amazing continuity of message from beginning to end.

The original language of the Old Testament is either Hebrew or Aramaic, a language very close to Hebrew. The oldest copies of the New Testament Scriptures that we have are in Greek. The Bible you are reading is an English translation from those original languages.

Throughout your Bible study, you will sometimes see *Word* capitalized. This refers to the Bible—the Word of God.

"All Scripture is God-breathed and is useful for teaching, rebuking, correcting and training in righteousness" (2 Timothy 3:16–17). Every truth that God has to impart is contained in the Scripture, which is His message to humanity.

Chapter 1

Delight in the Lord

"Delight yourself in the Lord and He will give you the desires of your heart" (Psalm 37:4).

I love the word *delight*. It is a happy word. It speaks of something beyond the usual pleasure. We get the words *delicious* and *delicacy* from the same root. Those English words come from a Latin root that means "to allure." Someone who delights you *draws* you. Someone who delights you is alluring, irresistible.

In whom do you delight? I delighted in my husband. I loved his company. I enjoyed his personality. I admired and respected him. His presence in my life brought me pleasure. Since his recent death, I delight in rich memories of him.

I delight in my children. I experience their joy and their pain as if it were my own. I invest my life in them because they are a delight to me. I find joy in doing those things that bring them joy. Because of the love I have for them, acts of duty seem like privilege. Things that in themselves would be drudgery to me, are instead outlets for my love. It is the relationship that changes duty to delight.

God has called me to delight in Him. The delight I have in my family is only a shadow of the delight I can find in God. His call is to a deeper level of delight than I can ever know in another human being. In responding to His call, my heart's cry becomes: "Whom have I in heaven but You? And besides You, I desire nothing on earth. My flesh and my heart may fail, but God is the strength of my heart and my portion forever. . . . But as for me, the nearness of God is my good" (Psalm 73:25–26; 28 NASB). I find Him so compelling, so alluring, that everyone and everything else pales in comparison to the pleasure of His presence.

In His presence, I am changed. The transforming power of His nearness reinterprets my world. In the light of His presence, circumstances may stay the same, but my interpretation is revolutionized. "Whatever was to my profit I now consider loss for the sake of Christ. What is more, I consider everything a loss compared to the surpassing greatness of knowing Christ Jesus my Lord, for whose sake I have lost all things. I consider them rubbish, that I may gain Christ" (Philippians 3:7–8).

Initially, I responded to His call to delight in Him to ensure the fulfillment of His promise to give me the desires of my heart. I had no idea that He would give me a new heart (Jeremiah 24:7). I didn't know that He would begin working in me to reproduce His own heart. When I turned to Him, I found that He Himself is my very great reward (Genesis 15:1). He is not, as I had supposed, the means to my end. Instead He is the desire of my heart.

If you are reading this book and you do not have that relationship with God that is available through Jesus Christ, then you won't be able to experience the truths this book presents. This is a book about a personal relationship in which prayer is the love language. Prayer is an interchange of love between the Father and His child. That desire you feel to pray is His love drawing you to delight in Him. You only need to respond. A simple explanation of how you can accept His gift of salvation is on page 160.

Delight in the Lord Through His Word

Delighting in the Lord is more than an emotion. Emotions will accompany the experience as it takes root in your life. You will come to feel great emotion and fervency toward God. But emotion is not the measure of your experience. We have many ways that we can work up feelings, but feelings don't last and feelings won't transform your desires. Emotions are unreliable. Emotions should follow, not lead. Emotions will eventually catch up to knowledge and understanding, but emotions should not be your compass.

The Hebrew word *delight* translated in Psalm 37:4 is from a root word meaning "soft and pliable." A paraphrase of this verse might be, "Become soft and pliable in God's hands, and He will mold your desires to match His." The apostle Paul wrote, "It is God who works in you to will . . . his good purpose" (Philippians 2:13). Delighting in the Lord changes you. It upgrades your desires, if I can use a techno-term. The things you want progressively change from shortsighted and short-term. Your desires are framed in eternity.

Scripture gives very explicit and practical instructions for how to delight in God.

Describing a righteous man, Psalm 1:2 says: "But his delight is in the law of the Lord, and on his law he meditates day and night." You can delight in the Lord by meditating on His Word.

God's revelation of Himself is spoken. His words reflect His character and reveal His heart. He will show Himself to you in the Bible, the record of His words. The Word, however, is more than the historical record of the sayings of God. The Word of God is living and active (Hebrews 4:12). God continues to speak His word, in present tense, to His people. Through the living power of His Holy Spirit within you, God personalizes His words to you. Chuck Swindoll, in his book *Simple Faith*, says that when we read the words of Scripture, they are so personal and so practical that "you would think the ink was still wet. They could have been written this very morning. In a sense they were . . . that's the way God's Word is, always alive and active and sharp."

For example, I read in Jeremiah 31:3, "'I have loved you with an everlasting love; I have drawn you with loving-kindness.'" If I read these as words He once spoke, I may learn intellectually that God uses kindness to draw people to Himself. I find new information about God. However, if I listen for God to speak His words to me, I hear, "Jennifer, I have loved *you* with an everlasting love; I have drawn *you* with loving-kindness."

As I hear His words in my spirit, I delight in Him. I am filled with awe that He would love me so. I rejoice in the sense of His loving presence speaking to me. I rest in the steadfastness of His love. I am reminded of His loving-kindness in the past and assured of His loving-kindness in the future. His Word produces reverence for Him. My faith is fed. My heart cries, "The law from your mouth is more precious to me than thousands of pieces of silver and gold" (Psalm 119:72). I'm different because I heard His word from His mouth.

When God speaks His Word to me, I leave the encounter changed. I have not received just a deeper understanding of His love, but a deeper experience of it. His Word is centered and anchored in my life through His Spirit. He teaches me. Great, high, God almighty teaches lowly me. "I have not departed from your laws, for *you yourself have taught me*" (Psalm 119:102).

The process of experiencing God, delighting in Him through His Word, is not instant. You must allow Him time. God unfolds His Word. He builds new understanding on previous under-standing. "The unfolding of your words gives light; it gives understanding to the simple" (Psalm 119:130). You must learn to meditate on His Word so that He can bring understanding. "'The meditation of my heart will be understanding'" (Psalm 49:3 NASB). Meditation is focused listening. It is coming before God, expecting Him to unfold His Word to you.

Meditation is not work. It is not applying all your intellectual pressure to squeeze meaning from Scripture. Meditation begins with God. As you consistently read God's Word, a phrase, or word, or thought seems to jump out at you. Something in your spirit responds and you sense that there is more there than you now know. Your spirit hungers for the understanding that lies just out of reach. This is God's initiative. This is God calling you to delight in Him by meditating on His Word.

Bring that phrase, word, or thought to Him and ask Him to unfold it to you. There are many ways to structure medita-tion, but be careful not to let the form take priority over the Fa-ther. Sometimes you might take the Scripture passage and rewrite it as God speaking it directly to you. Stop and consider every phrase or idea, then move on to the next. If another Scripture comes to mind and seems to add more depth of understanding, incorporate that into your writing. Read it over when you are finished. Be quiet in His presence and see what He will say to you. Always remember, your goal in meditation is not to understand theology, but to know God.

Other times you might want to come to God more simply, child to Father. You might state your desire for understanding, then wait quietly. For example, "Father, I don't really know what it means to die to myself. Will You show me?"

As you wait before Him, you may begin to recall recent events during which you insisted on your own way, proclaiming your right to your own opinion; you may begin to realize that the grudge you are holding against a neighbor is from wounded pride. As you wait before Him, you come to understand how alive your self-life is. Now you may change your question to ask, "Father, just how do I die to myself?" He will not give you a simple step-by-step answer. Over the next days or weeks, you may continually run across Scriptures during your Bible reading that shed new light and bring new insight. As circumstances occur, you are reminded of what you've learned in your meditation. You see God's Word reflected in your life. Little by little, God unfolds His Word to you about dying to self.

Sometimes meditation may take the form of adoration, simply considering God. For example, you may meditate on God as Creator. As you let your mind wander, the Holy Spirit's leadership may guide you to begin to think of the intricacies of creation. You may marvel at how every detail of creation works perfectly. You may be filled with wonder at the perfect functioning of the human body. Soon your mind turns to the Creator and you think of how easy it must be for One so imaginative and so powerful to work your circumstances together for good. Suddenly it is clear to you that worry is unnecessary. Your heart cries:

"May the glory of the Lord endure forever;
May the Lord rejoice in his works—he who looks at the earth, and it trembles, who touches the mountains, and they smoke.

I will sing to the Lord all my life;
I will sing praise to my God as long as I live.
May my meditation be pleasing to him, as I rejoice in the
Lord" (Psalm 104:31–34).

The results of meditation do not happen only in the time span allotted to meditating. That time only begins the unfolding process. You may continue to meditate on a single thought or passage for weeks or months or years. Meditation can occur in extended time periods, or during a few minutes of quiet.

A perfect time for meditation is the moments before sleep. "On my bed I remember you; I think of you through the watches of the night" (Psalm 63:6). Instead of thinking on the pressures tomorrow holds, or the stresses of the day just ending, center your thoughts on God. Let thoughts of Him fill your mind. Listen to His words. Psalm 16:7 says: " I will bless the *Lord* who has counseled me; indeed, my mind instructs me in the night" (NASB). In light of our current understanding of the processes of sleep, these words speak volumes. We know that the conscious, deliberative part of our mind goes into neutral during sleep. Our dreams are our subconscious minds working unhindered by our more inhibited conscious mind. Researchers have discovered that we can make deliberate use of our subconscious mind during sleep by being intentional about our thought processes before sleep. While we are sleeping, our subconscious mind can be meditating on the Word of God, finding new and delightful riches there. Did God mean this when He inspired David to pen this phrase? Consider the possibility of filling your thoughts with God's Word as you drift off to sleep. Go to sleep blessing the Lord, who counsels you, and let your mind instruct you in the night.

Make a conscious decision to delight in God by meditating on His Word day and night. What begins as a duty will become a privilege as your delight in Him grows. He will use His Word to mold your heart so that it matches His. Jesus said, "If you remain in me and my words remain in you, ask whatever you wish, and it will be given you" (John 15:7). As you make your heart's home in His Word, you will find your desires initiated and guided by Him. As His Word takes root in you, you will find He is watching over His Word to perform it (Jeremiah 1:12). You will find that the resources of heaven are at your disposal because "Your word, O Lord, is eternal; it stands firm in the heavens" (Psalm 119:89).

Delight in the Lord by Drawing Near

When you delight in someone, you desire that person's presence. You would not be satisfied to be separated from the person unnecessarily. You will go to great lengths to be together. My sons are all grown and living in other cities. When the opportunity presents itself, I will spend money to travel, rearrange my schedule, and expend my time and energy to see them. Whatever it takes to be in their presence, I will do. I delight in them.

Do you know why God has called you to delight in Him? Because He delights in you. He loves your presence. He has done what it takes to be present with you.

Shirley Dobson, in *Certain Peace in Uncertain Times,* writes, "He invites us into conversation with Him because it brings Him *pleasure.* That's sometimes a little hard to believe, isn't it? The holy and perfect and all-powerful ruler of the universe *enjoys* our prayers of praise? But the proof is in the Scripture: 'The prayer of the upright is His delight' (Proverbs 15:8 NKJV). God actually delights in and pursues our worship. As Jesus said, 'A time is coming and now has come when the true worshipers will worship the Father in spirit and in truth, *for they are the kind of worshipers the Father seeks*' (John 4:23)."

The presence of God delights the soul. "Surely you have granted him eternal blessings and made him glad with the joy of your presence" (Psalm 21:6). When Moses left his face-to-face encounters with God, his physical countenance reflected the glory of the presence of God. The skin of his face shone, and the sons of Israel were afraid to come near him (Exodus 34:30). The glory of God was mirrored in Moses' face. Moses had to hide God's glory by wearing a veil over his face until the shining had faded away because the children of Israel were unaccustomed to the presence of God.

The relationship between God and Moses occurred under the inadequacies of the Old Covenant.[1] Although God talked to Moses face-to-face, like a man talks to his friend, the Spirit of God did not indwell Moses as He does you. Moses' experience of the presence of God was less glorious than yours can be. Paul, in his second letter to the church at Corinth, makes this point: If the Old Covenant, which consisted of letters carved in stone, came with such glory that Moses' face shone from his encounter, won't the New Covenant, ministered by the Spirit, come in even more glory? (See 2 Corinthians 3:7–9.) You, child of the new, perfect covenant, can look directly at the glory of God, come boldly into His presence because Christ has opened the way. (See 2 Corinthians 3:18 and Hebrews 10:19–20.)

The presence of God is His gift to you. You are always in His presence. You don't move in and out of relationship with Him. He is always fully present to you, but you are not always fully present to Him. Train your thoughts to be aware of the ever-presence of God and to take delight in His nearness.

Look at what God has taught us about being in His presence. It is a privilege bought with a great price. It is not to be taken lightly. Look carefully at the picture Scripture paints. The tabernacle[2] was erected according to the detailed instructions given to Moses. It was to be a copy and shadow of spiritual realities (Hebrews 8:5). It was to be a visual aid to help us understand the truth.

The outer tabernacle was called the Holy Place (Hebrews 9:2). Numerous priests continually entered the outer tabernacle to perform their duties of worship and service (Hebrews 9:6). A veil separated the Holy Place from the Most Holy Place, the presence of God. Only the high priest entered the Most Holy Place, once a year, with blood that he offered for his own sins and the sins of the people (Hebrews 9:7). Free access to the presence of God was not available. Man was separated from God's presence by the veil. The sinful state of mankind is the true veil that deters free access to His holy presence.

Jesus inaugurated a new way into God's presence by fulfilling the Old Covenant, and thus putting into effect the New Covenant. In His flesh, His physical life, Jesus fulfilled the Old

Covenant's requirements for righteousness. The Old Covenant required sinlessness, which Jesus alone achieved. Having met the requirement of a perfect life, He could then fulfill the requirement of an unblemished sacrifice to atone for sin. Every condition of the Old Covenant was met. It is no longer in effect. Jesus said, "'Do not think that I have come to abolish the Law or the Prophets; I have not come to abolish them, but to fulfill them. I tell you the truth, until heaven and earth disappear, not the smallest letter, not the least stroke of a pen, will by any means disappear from the Law until everything is accomplished" (Matthew 5:17–18).

The theme of the Old Covenant is that the wages of sin is death. The theme of the New Covenant is that the gift of God is eternal life through Jesus Christ, His Son. Jesus is now the mediator of the New Covenant, a better covenant, which has been enacted on better promises (Hebrews 8:6). The mediator of a covenant acts on behalf of both parties to ensure that the terms of the agreement are fulfilled.

How does this relate to delighting in the presence of God? Now you can enter the Most Holy Place, the direct presence of God, "by a new and living way opened for us through the curtain, that is, his body" (Hebrews 10:20). Now you can draw near in the full assurance of faith (Hebrews 10:22) and experience firsthand the presence of God. Now God does not dwell in a tabernacle made with hands, but He dwells within you. The Most Holy Place is in you. You are no longer relegated to the outer tabernacle. You are now invited beyond the veil, to delight in His presence. In response, your heart cries, "You will fill me with joy in your presence, with eternal pleasures at your right hand" (Psalm 16:11).

To live in His presence is a privilege never to be taken for granted. Have you fully experienced this? Have you moved beyond the outer tabernacle in your prayer life? Are you still simply performing the service of prayer? Or have you known the delight of His presence? Just as Moses' face reflected the glory of God, so your life will reflect His presence. "And we, who with unveiled face all reflect the Lord's glory, are being transformed into his likeness with everincreasing glory, which comes from the Lord, who is the Spirit" (2 Corinthians 3:18).

As you behold His glory, you are changed so that your heart is a reflection of His. His concerns are your concerns. His desires are your desires. His will is reflected in your prayers. In His presence, your prayer life becomes consistently powerful and effective. This is not because you now have more influence on Him, but because He has more influence on you. The secret of prayer is not how to change God, but how to be changed by Him.

Receiving the Desires of Your Heart

Once you have learned to truly delight in the Lord, the desires of your heart are fulfilled. Now you are that one He seeks, whose heart is completely His. "For the eyes of the Lord range throughout the earth to strengthen those whose hearts are fully committed to him" (2 Chronicles 16:9). Prayer ceases to be the means by which you might bend God's will to yours, and becomes the process through which you assimilate His mind and heart. You can be mightily used by God in establishing His kingdom. With your heart at His disposal, He can set His plan in motion by planting a desire in your heart. You will experience boldness and confidence in prayer.

"This is the confidence we have in approaching God: that if we ask anything according to his will, he hears us. And if we know that he hears us—whatever we ask—we know that we have what we asked from him" (1 John 5:14–15).

Meditation

How tenderly You call my name, offering eternity; drawing me ever deeper into Your great heart. Like a magnet, Your irresistible pull is unrelenting. I surrender to Your gentle wooing, at last to find that You are my heart's cry.

"'Show me your face, let me hear your voice; for your voice is sweet, and your face is lovely" (Song of Songs 2:14).

Reflection

1. At this moment, what would you list as the desires of your heart?

2. Would you be willing to surrender those desires to God and allow Him, if need be, to recreate your heart's desires? If so, make that commitment now. Lay at His feet every desire of your heart. Write your thoughts down so that you will have a record of this commitment.

3. How would you describe your prayer life up to now? Have you experienced the level of delight in God to which He has called you? Are you satisfied with your prayer life?

4. Will you make a commitment to delight in God through meditating on His Word and living in His presence? If so, ask Him to direct your steps and show you the path of life. Worship Him and allow Him to impress upon you the great privilege of living beyond the veil. Thank Jesus for opening the way into the presence of God.

5. Stop and ask God to speak to you about delighting in Him. Write down what He says.

Review

1. What does it mean to delight in the Lord?

2. How can you learn to delight in the Lord?

3. How did Jesus open the way into God's presence?

4. What is the difference between the outer tabernacle and the Most Holy Place? What does that show you about your prayer life?

[1]The Bible divides God's revelation of Himself to man into two time frames, each marked by a covenant—a binding agreement between two parties. The dividing line between the two covenants is the Cross of Jesus. The Old Testament is the Scripture that represents the Old Covenant and the New Testament is the Scripture that describes the New Covenant. The apostle Paul says that the Old Covenant filled the role of a babysitter or a schoolteacher who would protect God's people from their own sinful inclinations until Christ came. Read Galatians 3:24-25. When Paul talks about "the Law," he means the Old Covenant. The Old Covenant was a covenant of laws to be obeyed. The laws were given for the people's benefit. The Law could not provide the power to obey, but could only motivate obedience through fear of punishment. It was never meant to be an eternal covenant. It was never called a perfect covenant. The New Covenant was put into effect when Jesus died for our sins and paid the penalty the Law demanded. He brought us into a new agreement, or covenant, with God. This covenant is eternal and perfect. In this covenant, the Law is put into our hearts and we have been given the Holy Spirit to empower us to obey. The punishment of every sin that we have ever committed or will ever commit has been paid for by the death of Jesus on the Cross. So the Law does not produce fear in us, but it produces love. If you would like to study this concept in more depth than this very brief description, you will find a list of resources in the back of this book.

[2]The tabernacle was the worship center for the nation of Israel as they traveled through the desert from Egypt to the Promised Land. It was a moveable temple. The presence of the Lord dwelt with His people in the tabernacle. The tabernacle had three areas: the outer courtyard where sacrifices were offered; the holy place, where the priests performed the rituals of worship that God commanded; and the Holy of Holies, where the presence of God dwelt. The Holy of Holies could be entered into only once a year and only by the high priest, who entered on behalf of the nation. On the Day of Atonement, a blood sacrifice was offered and the blood of that sacrifice was taken into the Holy of Holies by the high priest. There was a veil that blocked access to the Holy of Holies, the presence of God. When Jesus died on the Cross, that veil was torn in two from top to bottom. This indicated that the way into the presence of God had now been opened and that all who accepted the sacrifice of Jesus as their payment for sin, and who received Him as Lord of their lives, could enter the Holy of Holies. The Book of Hebrews, which you will find in the New Testament of your Bible, is written to people who had grown up in the Jewish faith and were steeped in the Law of the Old Covenant, but had now become followers of Jesus. The writer of Hebrews shows how the Old Covenant and the tabernacle were shadows of the reality that has come in Christ. If you want to understand more about this topic, you will find a list of resources in the back of this book.

Chapter 2

Pray Without Ceasing

"Pray without ceasing" (1 Thessalonians 5:17 NASB).

The admonition to pray without ceasing, which literally means without intermission, at first seems unrealistic. After all, one can't always be carrying on conversations with God. Other matters require attention. This dilemma brings you to the crux of the matter. What is prayer? Is prayer the words you direct to God? Is prayer an activity in which you are to engage on a regular basis? Is prayer a duty to be performed? Is prayer relegated to a specific time slot? Does prayer end with *Amen*?

Prayer is not an activity, but a relationship. Prayer is a relationship more intimate than any you can know with another person, because in prayer you draw on the life of Christ within you. During His earthly ministry, Jesus used several analogies to try to impart to us how complete our union with Him would be. Your life is to be so absorbed in His that you can say, "'I no longer live, but Christ lives in me'" (Galatians 2:20). Prayer is the unbroken flow of Christ's life in us that keeps us in the presence of God. It is Christ who makes intercession, not only *for* us, but *through* us.

Hebrews 7:25 tells us that Jesus "always lives to intercede for [us]." In John 14:16, Jesus says, "And *I will ask the Father*, and he will give you another Counselor to be with you forever." In

John 17:9, Jesus says, "I pray for them." The whole 17th chapter of John records Jesus's prayer for us. Jesus prays for us.

But Jesus also prays through us. Jesus has housed Himself in you; taken up residence in you (John 14:23). He says in Revelation 3:20: "Here I am! I stand at the door and knock. If anyone hears my voice and opens the door, I will come in and eat with him, and he with me." He will *come in* to the heart of the one who responds to His knock. He will come in and have fellowship and make Himself at home. If you are in relationship with Jesus, then He has made you His temple—the place where He dwells (1 Corinthians 3:16–17; 1 Corinthians 6:19; 2 Corinthians 6:16). If Jesus lives in you, and Jesus is praying, then Jesus is praying in you. He is reproducing His prayers in your heart.

> "There come times when prayer pours forth in volumes and originality such as we cannot create. It rolls through us like a mighty tide. Our prayers are mingled with a vaster Word, a Word that at one time was made flesh. We pray, and yet it is not we who pray, but a Greater who prays in us. . . . All we can say is, Prayer is taking place and I am given to be in the orbit." (Thomas R. Kelly, *A Testament of Devotion*)

> "The thought is tremendous. My friend, when you and I feel drawn to Prayer, it is God desirous of pouring forth His heart; the great depths of the thoughts of God—of His desires—seeking to find expression through such imperfect channels as you and me." (G. Granger Fleming, *The Dynamic of All Prayer*)

Prayer is often expressed in words, but it is not the words that God recognizes as prayer. It is not the cry of the lips, but the cry of the heart that God hears. We are living prayers. Our lives are the aroma of Christ rising before God continually as a sweet-smelling offering: "For we are to God the aroma of Christ" (2 Corinthians 2:15).

Chuck Swindoll says, "Prayer is making deliberate contact with God in word or thought. It is the voice of faith, whose whisper can be felt across the street or across the world. It is what pries us from our seats as spectators and places us as active participants with God."

The Vine's Life Through the Branch

Jesus used a word picture to make His point clear. "Remain in me, and I will remain in you. No branch can bear fruit by itself; it must remain in the vine. Neither can you bear fruit unless you remain in me. I am the vine; you are the branches. If a man remains in me and I in him, he will bear much fruit; apart from me you can do nothing" (John 15:4–5).

Jesus uses the word *remain*. He is emphasizing the permanent nature of the union. You are to live in Him and remain in Him, and He in you. He and you are so knit together, so one, that you are in Him and He is in you. This relationship is indissoluble. It cannot be undone. He states this again in John 17:21, 23, "Father, just as you are in me and I am in You. May they also be in us . . . I in them and You in me."

Do you remember your elementary school lessons in physical science? You learned the difference between a mixture and a solution. A mixture contains elements that are combined, but can be separated out again. Fruit salad is a mixture. A solution occurs when elements combine and become a new substance. Salt and water mix to form a solution because the salt dissolves in the water. The molecules in the two elements combine. They are no longer two elements, but one substance. Your life in Christ is not a mixture, but a solution. "Therefore if anyone is in Christ, he is a new creation" (2 Corinthians 5:17). Your life is dissolved in Christ's and you are a new being.

He is the vine and you are the branch. The source of the branch's life is the vine's life. The branch has no life of its own. If it is separated from the vine, it withers and dies and is good for nothing but firewood. However, if the branch remains in the vine, the branch bears fruit. The branch does not produce the fruit. The vine produces the fruit. The branch displays the fruit, evidence of the vine's life flowing through it. The branch can take no credit for the fruit it holds. The fruit brings glory to the vine. "Let your light shine before men, that they may see your good deeds and praise your Father in heaven" (Matthew 5:16).

The branch's one job is to abide. If the branch will abide, the vine will do all the work through it. Jesus gave two ways to abide in Him.

Abide in His Word

In John 15:7, Jesus said that to abide in Him, you must remain in His words and let His words remain in you. Remaining in His Word is more than reading your Bible a time or two each week. Jesus called you to soak yourself in His words. The Word of God nourishes your spirit just as food nourishes your body. Jeremiah said, "When your words came, I ate them; they were my joy and my heart's delight" (Jeremiah 15:16).

Your efficiently functioning digestive system knows how to use food to nourish your body. You don't have to be conscious of its functions. The nutrients from your food are absorbed into your bloodstream, which then deposits the right nutrients in the right cells. All this works without your conscious effort. All you have to do to fuel your body, to make it work most efficiently, is to ingest the proper foods. In the same way, your spirit knows how to digest and apply the Word of God. The Christ-life flowing through you will apply His words to your life. They will become for you a joy and the delight of your heart.

Suppose you were to look at an apple sitting on your kitchen counter. You might admire its shape and color. You might think about the nutrients it holds and consider the effect it would have on your body. But until you eat it and let it enter your body, all its potential is lifeless for you. Once you eat it, all the nutrients it contains come to life in you and are applied to your cells to impart their power.

The Word of God is not something that is applied to the surface of your life, for cosmetic purposes. It is to be taken into your life, where it can take root and nourish you from the inside out. His words begin to shape your thoughts and renew your mind.

When you abide in His Word, it becomes the mold in which your prayers are shaped.

Abide Through Obedience

"As the Father has loved me, so have I loved you. Now remain in my love. If you obey my commands, you will remain in my love, just as I have obeyed my Father's commands and remain in his love" (John 15:9–10).

Jesus said that you will abide in Him if you keep His commandments. He also said it this way: "'Whoever has my commands and obeys them, he is the one who loves me. He who loves me will be loved by my Father, and I too will love him and show myself to him" (John 14:21). Does this mean that you will be able to buy the love and presence of God through your good actions? Not at all. The love of God and the presence of Christ are realities, not changed by your feelings or perceptions. They are settled facts. What changes is your experience of His loving presence. Deliberate disobedience causes you to be less sensitive to Him.

His call to obedience is not a burden. Jesus says that His yoke is easy, and His burden is light (Matthew 11:30). He is calling you to live out your freedom, to make it real in your experience. Every command of His frees you from sin's destructive power. He wants you to live like the free person you are. His call to obedience is a call to freedom.

His life within you provides both the motivation and the power to obey: "It is God who works in you to will and to act according to his good purpose" (Philippians 2:13). The life of Christ can empower you from inside.

Within the context of your obedience, He can disclose Himself to you. He can be your prayer teacher. You can join Jesus in His intercession before the Father. He can pour His prayers through you.

The Flow of Christ's Life

"Then the Jews began to argue sharply among themselves, 'How can this man give us his flesh to eat?' Jesus said to them, 'I tell you the truth, unless you eat the flesh of the Son of Man and drink his blood, you have no life in you. Whoever eats my flesh and drinks my blood has eternal life, and I will raise him up at the last day. For my flesh is real food, and my blood is real drink. Whoever eats my flesh and drinks my blood remains in me, and I in him" (John 6:52–56).

Jesus shocked His listeners with these statements. "Many of his disciples said, 'This is a hard teaching. Who can accept it?'" (John 6:60). What did Jesus want us to understand? Why did He make this unsettling statement?

I believe that Jesus was trying to make this point: *Right now My life is outside you. The day will come when My life will be in you. You won't be able to follow Me as your leader, or role model. I must live My life through you. My life must be within you. I will take up permanent residence in you and exert My power in you continually.*

With the limited biological knowledge of His times, Jesus used the only picture He could to describe how something outside could get inside: eating and drinking. Perhaps today He would use the analogy of a blood transfusion.

My brother had leukemia. His blood could not perform its intended function because it was diseased. His blood could not cleanse and nourish his cells, but instead carried illness and death. When his disease was first diagnosed, it was announced throughout our community that Roger would need blood transfusions. When the bloodmobile was set up, people stood in line to give their healthy blood to replace his diseased blood. This, of course, was only a temporary measure because his bone marrow continued to manufacture diseased blood. Eventually his blood carried disease to all the organs of his body, and his body finally shut down. It all began in his blood.

"Life is in the blood" (Leviticus 17:11). A person's body may be functioning perfectly, but if the blood drains out, the body dies. There is no life without blood. If blood is healthy, it does just the opposite of diseased blood. Healthy blood carries oxygen to the body's cells and absorbs toxins. Healthy blood is cleansing and revitalizing to the body.

Think of the physical life as a picture of the spiritual life. We are born with an Adam-life, which is sin-diseased. The life which flows through our spiritual veins carries death. "'Those who live according to the sinful nature have their minds set on what that nature desires. . . . The mind of sinful man is death" (Romans 8:5-6).

The only remedy is to replace that diseased blood with healthy, life-giving blood. We will need to be transfused with the life of Christ.

This is the picture He was trying to give when He said that we must eat His flesh and drink His blood. He will live through you. His life will flow through you. You will be the instrument through which He expresses Himself to the world. You will not know Him from an outside source. You will know Him from inside, where He is always revealing Himself to you, always making His life available to you. It is no longer you who lives, but Christ who lives in you. The more you draw on His life that flows through you, the more His power becomes available to you.

Disobedience cuts off the flow of Christ's life as surely as a tourniquet cuts off the flow of physical blood. One of the functions of blood is to cleanse the body of toxins released by muscles as they work. When the flow of blood is cut off, the muscles may continue to work for a time, releasing toxins which are not washed away. Eventually those toxins build up, muscle use becomes painful, then impossible, infection sets in and the blood-deprived limb dies. If not amputated, the limb's infection will seep into the bloodstream and be carried throughout the body.

Disobedience is like tying a tourniquet around your spirit. At whatever point you are disobedient, the flow of Christ's life is restricted. Soon the poison building up in one area of your life will seep into all areas. Single acts of disobedience can't be isolated and kept from affecting your whole spiritual life. The process may be gradual, but unchecked disobedience will destroy you. It is His great love that calls you to obedience.

The blood of Christ, literally and physically shed on the Cross as payment for your sin-debt, is the ultimate testimony to His uncompromising, unflinching obedience. That power to obey is available to you through the One who lives in you.

This is what it means to pray without ceasing. Not to always be speaking words, but to live in a state of spiritual receptivity, always having Christ's life flowing through you, His heart beating in you. Are you beginning to see that prayer is more than a section of your life that can be cordoned off and isolated from the rest of life? Prayer is your spirit's life.

Unceasing Prayer

Pray without ceasing means to live in Christ and let Christ live in you. In this relationship, your life becomes a prayer, the sweet-smelling aroma of Christ to God. Unceasing prayer is living in the presence of God, beyond the veil. Paul says in Ephesians 2:6 that we are seated in the heavenly realms with Christ. The spiritual world is not limited by geographical location and the boundaries of place. If Christ is in you, and Christ is seated at the right hand of God, then you are seated with Him at the right hand of God. "Your life is now hidden with Christ in God" (Colossians 3:3). The kingdom of God, where spiritual laws are in effect, is within you. You can't reason this mystery based on physical principles. It is not a matter of being in two locations at one time, on earth and in heaven. Christ is in you, and you are in Christ, and Christ is in God. You are a living prayer.

Meditation

"Draw near, My child," is Your sweet call. My heart yearns to enter into Your beckoning Light. The services I have performed for You, the rituals to ensure Your favor, have left me empty. I can't seem to get beyond the veil, where the alluring brightness of Your glory shines.

Rest, abide. These are the mysteries. Your works won't show the way. Look to My Son. He is the Open Door into My presence. Lose yourself in Him to find your way to Me.

"See, I have placed before you an open door that no one can shut"
(Revelation 3:8).

Reflection

1. Right now, invite Jesus to transfuse you with His own life. Ask Him to show you any areas of disobedience that have cut off the flow of His life.

2. Renew your commitment to abide in His Word and to obey. State your trust in Him to reproduce His heart in you as you abide in Him.

3. Stop and listen. What is God saying to you? Write it down.

Review

1. What does it mean to pray without ceasing?

2. What does it mean to abide in Christ?

3. What does abiding in Christ have to do with your prayer life?

4. What are two ways to abide in Christ?

It has been such a blessing to be a part of a Moms in Touch prayer group. On the way to prayer one morning, I got a call from a mom who knows about our group but doesn't come. She called to ask us to pray for a boy facing surgery that day. I shared the request with our small group. One of the moms seemed perplexed and asked some questions. It turned out her husband was a neurosurgeon for the surgery. We prayed for the surgeon and the boy. The surgeon's wife went to the hospital and prayed with the family. Everything turned out well. It was just a blessing to me, most of all, I think, to see that I could be a part of what God has going on, through prayer.

When our group started out, none of us knew how to pray out loud. I think God's biggest work has been in us. We still are learning, but you can hear the heart's cry of each woman. These are not eloquent prayers, but when they are from the heart, God takes it from there.

Ruth E. Holding
Raleigh, North Carolina

Chapter 3

A Clean Heart

"Create in me a clean heart, O God, and renew a steadfast spirit within me" (Psalm 51:10 NASB).

"Who may ascend the hill of the Lord? Who may stand in his holy place? He who has clean hands and a pure heart" (Psalm 24:3–4).

"Blessed are the pure in heart, for they will see God" (Matthew 5:8).

"Let us draw near to God with a sincere heart in full assurance of faith, having our hearts sprinkled to cleanse us from a guilty conscience and having our bodies washed with pure water" (Hebrews 10:22).

A clean heart, or a pure, unadulterated heart, is a requirement for mountain-moving prayer. One whose heart is not clean can't enter into the intimate fellowship with the Father that He so desires. A heart with divided affections is a barrier between you and God. He is not satisfied with a halfhearted love. "Do not worship any other god, for the LORD, whose name is Jealous, is a jealous God" (Exodus 34:14). When God enters your life in His fullness, His presence sweeps clean every crack and crevice of your being.

Draw Near with a Sincere Heart

God invites you to draw near with a sincere heart. What is a sincere heart and how do you get one? The word *heart* is popularly used to indicate a mushy emotionalism: softhearted, brokenhearted, big-hearted, and so forth. However, when God refers to the heart, He is referring to the whole inner person. In its scriptural context, the heart is the seat of the intellect, the will, the personality, and the emotions. It would make sense to translate it as *mind*. The Father says, "Draw near with a sincere heart." A sincere, true, authentic, genuine heart is a heart that is what it purports to be. It is a heart that is unmixed, like pure gold or pure silver, unalloyed with other elements. Soren Kierkegaard has expressed it best: "Purity of heart is to will one thing." It is not the mighty in intellect who will see God, but the pure in heart.

You cannot purify your own heart. You do not have the ability to give God a sincere heart. Your heart is wicked and deceitful, and you cannot fully understand it. We are experts at deceiving ourselves with rationalizations and denials. Our hearts have an elaborate set of defense mechanisms that operate automatically to disguise our true selves. "The heart is deceitful above all things and beyond cure. Who can understand it?" (Jeremiah 17:9). Truth, or authenticity, is buried under layers and layers of pretense. We do not know the truth about ourselves. This is the human condition. We are helpless to even diagnose, let alone treat, our own desperate condition.

If God demands a pure heart, and you cannot achieve a pure heart, how will this dilemma be resolved? There is only one way to a pure heart—invite the Refiner's Fire into your life. "But who can endure the day of his coming? Who can stand when he appears? For he will be like a refiner's fire or a launderer's soap. He will sit as a refiner and purifier of silver; he will purify the Levites and refine them like gold and silver" (Malachi 3:2–3).

Silver is usually found in an ore alloyed with other, less valuable elements. The silver must be extracted and refined from all impurities to be considered pure silver. Impurities in a metal diminish its strength and dilute its value. By use of heat or chemicals, a refiner removes impurities and alloys so that pure silver is all that remains.

The Refiner's Fire enters your life as a heart-purifier. He refines you like silver. He isolates and then eliminates impurities. He washes you with launderer's soap. In biblical times, launderer's soap was used to clean clothing. Garments were soaked in launderer's soap to loosen the dirt and then stomped on to release the loosened grime.

Sometimes God uses adverse circumstances as a purifying agent. He may use the fiery heat of His holiness to convict you of sin and draw you toward righteousness. Every person and every circumstance He allows into your life can be used to purify you. Nothing is wasted, nothing is an accident. The purifying process, if momentarily painful or uncomfortable, is producing something eternal that far outweighs the temporary discomfort. "For our light and momentary troubles are achieving for us an eternal glory that far outweighs them all. So we fix our eyes not on what is seen, but on what is unseen. For what is seen is temporary, but what is unseen is eternal" (2 Corinthians 4:17–18).

Let me illustrate from my own life. I had been financially comfortable all my life. There were very few things I wanted that I could not afford. I thought I did not love material things. I thought I could be perfectly happy with or without them, that they did not add to my feeling of value. The truth was hidden and disguised by my deceitful heart. However, in the process of purifying me, God needed to expose the lurking, ugly reality.

My husband went through a long period of unemployment. Material things were unavailable to me. I found that I loved them very much. I found that my self-esteem was built on very shaky ground.

Not only does God want to expose impurities, but He also wants to remove them. As He brought my problem to the surface in the crucible of my circumstances, He also began to clean it away. He did that by allowing me to experience His love and care with such clarity that I saw everything else in a new light. For two years, nothing changed in my circumstances, but everything changed in my perception. He thrust a circumstance on me so that He could build a sincere heart within me.

This is only one example. Many times God has used people and circumstances to cause me to come face-to-face with the truth.

He continues to build authenticity into my life. Although it is a difficult transition, He causes me to love the truth more than the lie. My first reaction is to hide from the truth and cling to the lie. The lie always makes me look better to myself. At first, I always love the darkness more than the light. I feel exposed in the light. And then He reminds me that He is the Light and the Truth, and that He has come to set me free. It is His great mercy and love for me that brings Him into my life as the Refiner's Fire.

I am learning to welcome tribulation and to treat it as a friend. Trials are God's detergents. He works in me to create the desire for Him, whatever the cost. "Not only so, but we also rejoice in our sufferings, because we know that suffering produces perseverance; perseverance, character; and character, hope. And hope does not disappoint us" (Romans 5:3–4). It is His mighty power in my inner person that is burning away everything that is not Him, every rival for my affections, causing me to will one thing. This refining and purifying has one goal: to free me to be what I am called to be. "Not that I have already obtained all this, or have already been made perfect, but I press on to take hold of that for which Christ Jesus took hold of me" (Philippians 3:12). And for what purpose did Christ take hold of me? To establish the kingdom of God on earth through prayer. The Master teaches me to pray, "Thy kingdom come. Thy will be done, on earth as it is in heaven."

Draw Near with a Heart Sprinkled Clean

God wants us to draw near with a heart sprinkled clean from an evil conscience. The phrase *sprinkled clean* refers to the Old Covenant requirements of being cleansed by blood. The sprinkling of blood inaugurated the Old Covenant (Hebrews 9:18-22) and was used consistently throughout the Old Testament to signify cleansing. Again, drawing on modern understanding of human physiology, we know that blood does not cleanse from the outside, but from the inside.

Blood is the essence of life. It is because the blood represents the vitality, the life and being, that it makes atonement. "'For the life of a creature is in the blood, and I have given it to you to make atonement for yourselves on the alter; it is the blood that makes atonement for one's life'" (Leviticus 17:11). The blood of Christ represents His life force, His Holy Spirit, which flows through our spirits, cleansing us. "And the blood of Jesus, his Son, purifies us from all sin'" (1 John 1:7). You are continuously being cleansed of all unrighteousness because He lives His life through you. His life is always flowing through you, flushing away impurities.

As our blood flows through our physical bodies, it carries away toxins. When God instituted the New Covenant, He changed His whole theater of operation from outside man to inside man. His law is not written on stone tablets, but on the tablets of the heart. The blood which sealed the first covenant was the blood of animals. It could not really cleanse, but could only symbolize cleansing. The only way for that blood to be applied was by sprinkling it externally. The blood of the eternal covenant is the blood of Christ. His blood—His life, in Spirit form, is not sprinkled on, but flowing through. The cleansing life flow has been transfused into us.

The life Christ lives through you is not the life He once lived in the flesh, encapsulated in time. He lives His resurrected life in you; His present-tense life, His glorified life. He does not diminish Himself to fit your limitations, but He expands you to accommodate His unlimited capacities. In letting go of the Adam-life to embrace the Christ-life, you learn that you can do all things through Christ who strengthens you. I don't mean that you are all-powerful and can do anything you set out to do. I mean you are empowered to do anything God appoints you to do. He will call on you to do far more than you could ever do in your own power.

The uninterrupted flow of Christ's life through you keeps you in unbroken fellowship with the Father. His cleansing is always active within you. He is always working in you to create a clean heart.

Experiencing a Clean Heart

To experience a clean heart, a sincere heart, you must willingly submit yourself to God for the purpose of having sin exposed and expunged. You must come to the conclusion that you cannot purify your own heart, that you are helpless in this matter. This is an important part of the faith journey. God gave the law for just this purpose.

The law is to have two functions in the life of the believer. First, the law shows you your sin by clarifying the standard of righteousness. "I would not have known what sin was except through the law. For I would not have known what coveting really was if the law had not said, 'Do not covet'" (Romans 7:7).

Second, the law exposes your powerlessness over sin. In seeking to keep the law, you will fail time and again. You will be unable to live up to God's standard. "I know that nothing good lives in me, that is, in my sinful nature. For I have the desire to do what is good, but I cannot carry it out" (Romans 7:18).

Have you reached this conclusion? Do you know for certain that, no matter how firm your purpose or how good your intentions, you cannot fulfill the standard of righteousness? Have you given up?

Giving up is hard. It's hard to admit that you're powerless. It's even harder to relinquish your whole self, which is required for a pure heart.

Let me explain what I mean. I want to be cleansed of my sins. My sins are inconvenient to me. They show me for what I am. They diminish my life. I want God to come into my life and patch up the holes and put on a new coat of paint. I want my life to look bright and shiny and to feel good. But that's not His way.

Do I want Him to tear down the old and build something new? Do I want to die to myself and live to Him? Do I want Him to deal with the very root of my sins, my self-rule? He wants to take out my old heart and put in a new heart. My old heart, my Adam-life, is set on my gain. At its very best, no matter how good my actions, how righteous my thoughts, my heart is set on my gain. I come to God for His favors, for His blessings, for His forgiveness, for my own sake. No matter how much I want to change, I can't. I can't change my heart.

"I will give you a new heart and put a new spirit in you; I will remove from you your heart of stone and give you a heart of flesh. And I will put my Spirit in you and move you to follow my decrees and be careful to keep my laws" (Ezekiel 36:26–27).

A heart transplant. A blood transfusion. A completely new creation. This is the radical work of Christ in me. This is the New Covenant way. Free from the external law, bound to the "living law." The law once engraved on stone, now engraved in my inner person.

Now everything is changed. The law is not a document, but a person. Jesus is the embodiment of the law. His life is flowing through you. The law is not a burden to which you are bound or by which you are inhibited. Rather He is the freedom you are seeking. He is the escape from the sin that had bound you. As you live your daily life, the living law within guides you. It is the Holy Spirit who makes the law real in your experience.

To experience this life, you must be always yielded and receptive. You must accept your own helplessness and inability to change. Once you've learned the ways of God, you can, like Paul, boast about your weaknesses, that the power of Christ may dwell in you. Be well content with your weaknesses, for when you are weak, then you are strong.

"But he said to me, 'My grace is sufficient for you, for my power is made perfect in weakness.' Therefore I will boast all the more gladly about my weaknesses, so that Christ's power may rest on me. That is why, for Christ's sake, I delight in weaknesses, in insults, in hardships, in persecutions, in difficulties. For when I am weak, then I am strong" (2 Corinthians 12:9–10).

In other words, at the points of your weakness the power of Christ will be most evident. Instead of defining yourself by what you can do, you will define yourself by what Christ can do. Your inability to achieve a clean heart is not a defeat, but a victory. Now God can do His mighty work without interference from you. Now His power can show itself through your weakness.

To experience a clean heart, first yield yourself to God to do His work in you in His way. Then, in your scheduled prayertimes, allow time for confession and cleansing. In this time, it is not your responsibility to dredge up your faults. You should not be looking inward, but upward. God will talk to you about the issues on His mind. As God shows you an issue, agree with Him and repent. Claim His power for that weakness. This process is not accomplished in one sitting. The more deeply rooted the sin, the more time it will take. Let God work. Finally, in walking with God in unbroken fellowship, listen and obey moment by moment.

"Whether you turn to the right or to the left, your ears will hear a voice behind you, saying, 'This is the way; walk in it'" (Isaiah 30:21).

Scripture gives a picture of the prayer warrior's purified heart. In Malachi 3:3 we are told that the Messiah will be a refiner and purifier of silver. Silver has several qualities that God wants to produce in you. Silver is the most malleable of all metals. It can be easily hammered into new shapes. God does not want you to harden your heart. He wants to be able to shape and mold your heart until it looks exactly like His. Like a purifier of silver, He will remove everything that causes your heart to be hard.

Silver is the best conductor of electricity and heat. When a conductor is charged with electricity by absorbing electrons from an electrically charged source, it holds those electrons until it touches another conductor that has not been charged. Then the electrons move between the charged conductor and the uncharged so that the electrical charge is spread over both conductors. As intercessors, we are to be conductors of God's life. We receive His life and pass it on. Any impurities in silver lessen its effectiveness as a conductor.

Silver reflects light better than any other element. Many mirrors are made by putting a thin layer of silver onto a sheet of high-quality glass. God wants to purify our hearts so that they reflect His heart perfectly.

Silver is the metal most resistant to corrosion from the atmosphere. God wants to create an incorruptible heart in His intercessors. He wants a heart that is not conformed to the world, but transformed by the Spirit (Romans 12:2).

Draw near to God with a genuine heart, in the full assurance of faith, and with a heart cleansed by the blood of Christ. This is the heart of an intercessor.

Meditation

My child, let Me do My work in you. Let Me free you from yourself. Let Me show you that your truest self, your highest self, is yet to be.

Not in anger will I refine you, but in love greater than you can conceive.

Come to Me in the full assurance of faith. Rest here. Rest from all your futile attempts at purity. Let Me display My strength through your weakness. Let Me do what you cannot.

"'I will give them a heart to know me, that I am the Lord'" *(Jeremiah 24:7).*

Reflection

1. Ask God: *Father, is there anything that is keeping me from being the prayer warrior that You intend me to be?* Listen.

2. Is God at work refining you right now? Have you surrendered yourself to that process? Will you stop resisting God's refining work and give Him complete access to your life?

3. Will you give up all attempts to change your own heart and let the Holy Spirit accomplish everything?

4. Listen to what God is saying right now. Write it down.

Review

1. What is a pure heart?

2. How is a pure heart attained?

3. Why did God use silver to represent a purified heart?

4. How does a pure heart relate to prayer?

God has been faithful to a weekly group praying at my kitchen table or at our Christian school or at a friend's table for more than ten years.

One of the people who prayed with our group had a son who was my son's best friend. This young man died tragically at the age of 15, with my son and many others present at his death. His parents were devastated. Our group prayed daily at their house for about six weeks as this family began to be healed. God's presence was undeniable. It was the most heartbreaking, amazing time of prayer for us who, by this time, knew well how to pray in one accord and how to hurt in one accord.

Jennie Alexander

Chapter 4

He Who Loves Me

"'Whoever has my commands and obeys them, he is the one who loves me. He who loves me will be loved by my Father, and I too will love him and show myself to him" (John 14:21).

Obedience is the door to revelation. The only way to know the mind and will of God is for Him to reveal it to you. Praying according to God's will is the only way to know that you will receive what you ask for. "This is the confidence we have in approaching God: that if we ask anything according to his will, he hears us. And if we know that he hears us—whatever we ask—we know that we have what we asked of him" (1 John 5:14–15).

Obedience and prayer go hand in hand. "We . . . receive from him anything we ask, because we obey his commands and do what pleases him" (1 John 3:21–22).

You don't pray for the purpose of informing God. Rather, God tells you to call to Him so that He can show you great and mighty things that you have not known (Jeremiah 33:3). The beginning point of prayer is hearing from God. You can't live in disobedience and hear God clearly. Disobedience dulls your spiritual senses. Disobedience short-circuits prayer at its source.

Prayer is more than the words you speak. There have always been people who spoke much love, but their heart was set on their gain. There have always been those who spoke in His name, but He never knew them. Jesus said it clearly: The one who loves Me is the one who obeys Me, the one whose words and actions match.

Because He knows the thoughts and intentions of the heart, because we are laid bare before Him, we cannot placate Him with words of love. He calls for that love to be lived out through obedience. "This is love for God: to obey his commands. And his commands are not burdensome" (1 John 5:3–4).

Obedience Stems from a Pure Heart

The inner change affected by the Holy Spirit will manifest itself outwardly in your conduct. Your inward purity and outward obedience intertwine. The Holy Spirit is responsible for both, "'for it is God who works in you to will and to act according to his good purpose" (Philippians 2:13).

The inner transformation is achieved by the Holy Spirit, requiring only your attention and willingness to yield to Him. The outer manifestation requires that you live out the inner change in actions empowered by the Holy Spirit. "Therefore, my dear friend, as you have always obeyed . . . continue to work out your salvation with fear and trembling, for it is God who works in you to will and to act according to his good purpose" (Philippians 2:12–13). Here Paul links the two seemingly opposite thoughts. Paul's injunction to work out your salvation does not mean to work for your salvation. The eternal salvation of your soul is secure, a free gift from God through Christ. However, this eternal salvation, or deliverance from sin, will show up in daily salvation. To work it out means to complete or fulfill it, bring it from the inside to the outside. This will require your active participation. Even your active participation is empowered by God. He is the power to be and the power to do.

Obedience Stems from a Personal Relationship

The obedience to which you are called is not a rule-following obedience. There is no formula. Obedience will call for different things from different people. Jesus's exchange with Peter before His ascension makes this clear. After telling Peter how he would die, Jesus issued the challenge: "Follow Me!" Peter turned around and saw John. "Lord," asked Peter, "what about him?" Jesus's reply was, "'If I want him to remain alive until I return, what is that to you? You must follow Me!" (See John 21:18–22.) Peter's obedience would look different than John's obedience. Your obedience will look different than someone else's obedience. The wonderful relationship you have with Jesus is a living thing, a dynamic and daily interaction. You follow Him.

Obedience springs from an ongoing relationship with God through Christ, managed and maintained by the Holy Spirit. To obey, you must be able to hear; to hear, you must be living in the full assurance of faith. How are faith and obedience connected?

Faith is your capacity to receive spiritual information. "Faith comes from hearing the message, and the message is heard through the word of Christ" (Romans 10:17). The beginning point of faith is hearing the word of Christ. What level of hearing will give birth to faith? Hearing in the heart, with spiritual ears. Two people can hear the same words with their physical ears. One will be unaffected, having heard in word only. The other will be transformed, filled with faith, having heard in power and in the Holy Spirit. (See 1 Thessalonians 1:5.)

When the Word of God is declared to you from within, faith will accompany it. The Word of God is living and active. There will be an inner certainty. Obedience is hearing with the ears of faith when the Master says, "You follow Me!" Receiving the message in power and in the Holy Spirit means that the message finds its target in your heart. The message you hear is not general, but specific and personal. Faith has made it so.

"By faith Abraham, when he was called, obeyed" (Hebrews 11:8 NASB). Where did Abraham's faith begin? With God's call. How was it manifested? In Abraham's obedience. The key here, missed by so many Christians today, is that God is to be the primary source of information about Himself. We are blessed today with an abundance of wonderful preachers, Bible teachers, and writers. Yet, trying to build faith on the words of people, even when those words are true, is futile. You must hear directly from

God. Otherwise you are just collecting information. People may speak words, but the Holy Spirit speaks revelation. God may use great communicators to speak to you, but He doesn't need them. He is within you. His words are engraved on your inner being. You are not dependent on any outside source for revelation. The Living Word, the full revelation of God, is your life. Listen to Him. Follow Him. Don't be satisfied with following the rules. Follow the Ruler.

If you have just been collecting information, then the more you learn, the more burdened and guilty you feel. God's voice does not come in generalities, but in specifics. Moment by moment and step-by-step, guiding and empowering.

No one has more access to God than you do. "The Lord would speak to Moses face to face, as a man speaks with his friend" (Exodus 33:11). Now let the Holy Spirit speak to you: "As I was with Moses, so I will be with you" (Joshua 1:5). Let the Holy Spirit work that truth into your life. The vibrancy of the relationship is due to the intimacy nurtured in the communication between your heart and His.

Obedience Brings Freedom

"I will walk about in freedom, for I have sought out your precepts" (Psalm 119:45).

We, as a society, have a distorted view of freedom. In general, we think of freedom as the ability to make our own choices without interference from an outside source. Freedom goes much deeper than that. Even if you could free yourself from every outside master, you would be enslaved to your own nature.

As a human being in a fallen world, you were born into slavery. Physically, you were born with a genetic blueprint that would determine the color of your eyes, the texture of your hair, the shape of your face, and more. Spiritually, you were born with a genetic blueprint that predetermined slavery. Mankind is enslaved to the impulses of human nature, the independent self, the Adam-life. Jesus said, "'Everyone who sins is a slave to sin'" (John 8:34). Paul gave this admonition: "Therefore do not let sin reign in your mortal body so that you obey its evil desires. Do not offer the parts of your body to sin, as instruments of wickedness. . . . Don't you know that when you offer yourselves to someone to obey him as slaves, you are slaves to the one whom you obey—whether you are slaves to sin, which leads to death, or to obedience, which leads to righteousness" (Romans 6:12–13, 16).

In this context the *sin* that reigns is not specifically the sinful actions we commit. Rather, it is the root of sin that forms our human nature. Sin, as defined by Scripture, is not an arbitrary list of bad things that annoy God. Sin is that which limits our potential. Sin enslaves us to the self–destructive behaviors and thought patterns that are our heritage as humans. All sinful acts, which are results of the root of sin, are inherently destructive to us. That's what defines them as sin. Sin becomes addictive in a sense. Actions or attitudes that we first entered into freely, later enslave us. Even after seeing their destructive effects, we seem unable to free ourselves. Jesus stated that His mission was not to condemn sinners, but to deliver them. "For God did not send his Son into the world to condemn the world, but to save the world through him" (John 3:17). It is not an angry, petty, vindictive God who warns that the wages of sin is death, but our loving Father sounding the alarm.

In this passage from Romans, Paul says that you will be a slave of something—either sin or righteousness. When you were a slave of sin, Paul reasons, you were free in regard to righteousness. But what good did that do you? You were bringing on your own destruction. True freedom is found in being a slave of righteousness. "For the wages of sin is death, but the gift of God is eternal life in Christ Jesus our Lord" (Romans 6:23).

Every act of obedience is a step toward greater freedom. For example, Jesus said, "When you stand praying, if you hold anything against anyone, forgive him" (Mark 11:25). This is a difficult thing to obey because our spiritual genetics predispose us to hold a grudge or exact revenge. The command to forgive everyone for everything opposes our human nature. This command to forgive seems like a heavy burden to bear. It seems too much to ask.

Having heard the command of Christ, you are now faced with a choice. Will you be a slave to anger and bitterness, which will lead to your own destruction? Or will you forgive and be freed from the too-heavy, emotionally crippling burden of anger? Will you draw on the resources of your old self, or will you draw on the resources of the kingdom of God? You choose.

I want to explore the issue of forgiveness because it is a command directly tied to prayer. There are many levels of offense, all of which must be forgiven for your own good. However, I know that some of you reading this book have been betrayed or abused and are suffering great inner pain. That pain may be intensified by feelings of guilt brought on by knowing you should be able to forgive. Remember several things.

Forgiveness is a process. It is not accomplished by saying a few magic words. It is a process initiated and completed by Christ in you. You do not have a deadline to meet. Your process may be different from anyone else's. You may be encouraged or guided by the similar experiences of others, but don't be dictated to by them. Be patient with yourself. Remember that God has undertaken the work within you and the responsibility is His. Once you have entered the process by yielding yourself to His working, you have fulfilled His commandment. You can't begin the process until you can face your anger and hurt honestly. Let me quote Carole E. Smith, MS, MA, of the Atlanta Counseling Center:

"We cannot know God fully until we know who we are and what has formed us. We do not go to God despite the sin perpetrated upon us. We go to God because of it, and we must take it to God held in both hands, known by heart and seen with both eyes. That is when we can hand it over. That is when we can forgive our abusers.

"Yet, many Christians today seem intent on stressing that there is a quicker route to God, that there are steps that will lift us up and over sin and pain, that we can pray and forgive another without ever knowing or examining the imprint that sin had on our lives. Such is resurrection without crucifixion. It is Bonhoeffer's 'cheap grace': a magic carpet to recovery that sounds right but never gets off the ground."[1]

Don't be afraid to take your pain and anger to God. He won't reject you. He is not fragile. You can ask Him your hardest questions. You can lay your blackest anger out before Him, even when some of that anger is directed at Him. He will take you by the hand and walk you step-by-step through the process of forgiveness and inner healing. He will put all the pieces back together again. As He does, He will show you Himself in new and wonderful ways. He will use even the most awful events for your good. Your pain and the subsequent healing and transformation will make you into a powerful intercessor.

When God leads you through fire, it is not a destroying fire, but a cleansing fire. It will not burn you. It will refine you. He is shaping you, like an artist shapes a sculpture. The fire will set the work He has done so the shape will be stable. Never be afraid of the fire.

Obedience Increases Your Delight in the Lord

"I desire to do your will, O my God; your law is within my heart" (Psalm 40:8). Because God has created you and has set out a purpose for your life, obedience brings a sense of fulfillment. Because His law is within you, obedience brings harmony to your life. Obedience harmonizes your inner longings and your actions. You are being what you are created to be and doing what you are created to do. As you take each step of obedience, the next step is revealed. Your faith grows with each experience. Life becomes a joyous adventure.

Jesus told His disciples to obey Him, just as He had obeyed His Father. Then He said, "'I have told you this so that my joy may be in you and that your joy may be complete'" (John 15:11). Obedience, both in the overall moral conduct of your life and in the moment-by-moment obedience, increases intimacy. In obeying, you are drawing near to God, and He is drawing near to you. Disobedience erects barriers. Obedience bonds you more closely to the Father, who has written His law on your heart.

God's call to obedience is a result of how much He loves you and how tenderly He watches over you, careful not to let you go on in actions that He knows will keep you from reaching your potential. During my husband's illness, I saw a picture of God's loving call to obedience. I wrote this in my journal:

Today as I sat beside Wayne's hospital bed, I watched a parable in action.

Wayne is being fed and medicated by IV right now. Lots of tubes acting as the conduit through which life and healing flow. Wayne is very restless. He keeps moving his arm in such a way that the IV lines get tangled and the healing flow can't get to him. When he starts moving his arm too much, we have to take his hand and gently hold it down so he won't get the lines tangled. It frustrates him. He feels we are restricting his freedom. He is missing the context. All he knows is he wants his hand to move and we want it to be still. He can't see that what he thinks is restriction is really freedom—freedom to receive the flow that sustains his life. Like Wayne, we often chafe at God's call to obedience, thinking it restricts us. Our view is narrow. We can't see that His loving hand on ours is freedom. It keeps us in the place where His power and provision flow. It keeps us from moving out of the flow of His life. This morning when I got to Wayne's room, they had tied that restless hand to the bed with just enough give that he had freedom, but not license. In other words, he could move his hand, but only within the confines of that which was safe for him. It was a comfortable, soft little cuff around his wrist, but it surprised me and hurt me when I saw it. I thought, how much better when the discipline comes from a loving hand. How much better when that "restriction" is accompanied with a loving touch and gentle words instead of in a impersonal "law" that has no heart. See how much God loves us? His guidance comes to us from His loving hand, accompanied by His gentle voice, until we learn by experience that His commands set us free.

"I run in the path of your commands, for you have set my heart free"
(Psalm 119:32).

Obedience Involves Risk

God will call for obedience at the place where you are most securely tied to the kingdom of the world. He will call on you to risk everything to follow Him. When the rich young ruler came to Jesus inquiring about eternal life, Jesus first told him to keep the commandments. The young man stated that he had kept all the commandments. "Jesus answered, 'If you want to be perfect, go, sell your possessions and give to the poor, and you will have treasure in heaven. Then come, follow me.' When the young man heard this, he went away sad because he had great wealth" (Matthew 19:21–22).

The rich young ruler would do almost anything to have eternal life. Almost. Jesus saw through all his goodness, his rulekeeping, to what possessed his heart. That was the obedience Jesus required. Jesus wanted the young man to divest himself of that which occupied the place only God should hold. Jesus wanted the young man to move his faith and confidence from his possessions to the Father. The rich young ruler wouldn't take the risk.

Contrast that with the similar challenge to Abraham. Genesis 22:1 says that God tested Abraham. He called on Abraham to take Isaac, "your son, your only son, whom you love" and offer him as a sacrifice. We can imagine Abraham's feelings. His only son, doubly precious because he was the child of promise, the living, breathing proof of God's faithfulness. Isaac was God's only possible rival in the heart of Abraham. Abraham knew God had given Isaac for His purpose. He did not understand the obedience being required of Him, but he knew God. Abraham risked the one he loved most, fully confident that God would be able to restore him, even from the dead.

Obedience for Mary meant risking her reputation. As a result, she is called blessed among women (Luke 1:42). Obedience for Abraham meant risking his security. As a result, he received a city whose building and architect is God. Obedience for Paul meant risking his position. As a result, the gospel was spread to the Gentile world.

Sometimes we get the idea that only the "big" acts of obedience matter. But an obedient heart, a habit of obedience, is cultivated in the small daily moments. Unless you learn obedience in the dailiness of relationship, you will not be equipped to respond in obedience to the big challenges.

What is God calling on you to risk? What are you afraid to lay on His altar? Will you risk everything on the grace of God? He is calling you to revelation. He is calling you to abide in His love. He is calling you to experience His life. God is calling you to uncompromising obedience—obedience in the small things and in the big things.

Meditation

Follow Me. Live My life in your world. Express My love. Speak My words. You are My chosen instrument. You are living proof that I Am.

"Today if you hear His voice, do not harden your hearts"
(Hebrews 4:7).

Reflection

1. As you read this chapter on obedience, what did God spotlight in your life? Remember, God does not call you to see your sin except against the backdrop of His grace. "Where sin increased, grace increased all the more" (Romans 5:20). He does not want to condemn you, but deliver you. Are you willing to confess and forsake the disobedience He has pinpointed?

2. Will you place yourself in the custody of the Holy Spirit? He will empower you to act out your inner transformation.

3. What is God calling on you to risk in obedience to Him? Will you place it on His altar right now?

4. What have you heard from God? Write it down.

Review

I. How are obedience and prayer connected?

2. What is the relationship between a pure heart and obedience?

3. What is the relationship between a personal relationship with God and obedience?

4. How does obedience bring freedom?

5. How does obedience involve risk?

[1]Carole E. Smith, Atlanta Counseling Center (Atlanta: Atlanta Counseling Center, Spring 1991), 1–2.

Years ago, maybe in my teenage years, I developed a pattern of either saying or thinking when someone asked me to pray for their specific need that I would be glad to "stand in the gap" on their behalf.

It was in the fall of 2005 that I felt God tugging at my heart to start a GAP group. As I prayed about this and trusted God for insight and direction, GAP became an acronym for Grandmothers Are Praying. Many of my family and friends supported me in prayer and encouraged me with their words as I set out to launch GAP. It has been amazing! There were seven of us who met to share our hearts and our requests with our Father who promises to hear our cries. I believe the greatest benefit of that day was knowing that we would be standing in the gap for each grandmother's request until we could chart the path God had planned to answer our requests.

Snookie Barnett
Rockwall, Texas

Chapter 5

Pray in the Spirit

"Pray in the Spirit on all occasions with all kinds of prayers and requests" (Ephesians 6:18).

It is through the Holy Spirit that the life of Christ is operative within you. He is Christ's life transfused into you and flowing through you. He is the One who makes the thoughts of God known to you. True prayer cannot happen apart from the Spirit of God.

What does it mean to pray in the Spirit? I believe that we can't understand this concept until we know what it means to be filled with the Spirit. Throughout the New Testament, we are told to live by the Spirit (Galatians 5:16), wait for our hope through the Spirit (Galatians 5:5), be led by the Spirit (Romans 8:14), keep in step with the Spirit (Galatians 5:25), obey through the Spirit (1 Peter 1:2). We are to live every aspect of our lives through the Spirit.

Jesus lived His earthly life in the Spirit's power. He was full of the Holy Spirit after His baptism and was led by the Spirit in the wilderness when He was tempted by the devil (Luke 4:1). After His time of testing, He returned to Galilee in the power of the Spirit (Luke 4:14). He opened His ministry by declaring, "'The Spirit of the Lord is on me'" (Luke 4:18). He offered Himself without blemish to God through the power of the eternal Spirit (Hebrews 9:14). Jesus lived every moment on earth connected to the Father through the Spirit.

The Holy Spirit is in control of every aspect of your salvation. He convicted you of sin and drew you to Christ. He made the message of salvation clear to you. The moment you received Christ as your personal Savior, you received the Holy Spirit. "'If anyone does not have the Spirit of Christ, he does not belong to Christ'" (Romans 8:9). The Holy Spirit is God's guarantee of your relationship with Him. "In Him, you also, after listening to the message of truth, the gospel of your salvation—having also believed, you were sealed in Him with the Holy Spirit of promise" (Ephesians 1:13 NASB). "We know that we live in him and he in us, because he has given us of his Spirit" (1 John 4:13).

You are sealed in Christ, Paul writes in Ephesians 1:13. Sealed like a letter is sealed in an envelope. You are stamped with God's personal seal, thereby stamped as truly one of His own. In the days of Paul, a person sending a letter would set his own seal on it. This seal was the guarantee that the letter was genuine. It was the authenticating mark. The Holy Spirit seals you in Christ and is the authenticating mark of God. The Holy Spirit abides continually in you. Your access to the power and riches of God is equal to anyone who has ever lived. You have the same Holy Spirit that any of the great men and women of the Bible had. The very same.

Being Filled with the Spirit

Is being filled with the Spirit something more than having received the Spirit at salvation? In many lives, there is a time at which the reality of the Holy Spirit's indwelling brings on the understanding with new power. Many people whose names you will never know have experienced this, as have many whose names are instantly recognizable. George Mueller, Dwight L. Moody, Peter Marshall, Andrew Murray, Hudson Taylor, R. A. Torrey, Rees Howells to name a few, are men mightily used by God, who reached a crisis moment in their lives during which they surrendered more fully to the indwelling Christ, the Holy Spirit. Afterward, each testifies to a new power in ministry, a new victory over sin, a new sense of uninterrupted peace. Each person's experience is different. Some report that their experience was very emotional. Others don't have a particular feeling or emotion at all. There is no formula. A full surrender to the Holy Spirit's work in your life is entirely personal.

My friend, Chris, lived in fear of her life every day. She grew up in a Christian home, had known Christ as her Savior since childhood, was active in her church, and knew everything about God she could know. Still, she could not escape fear. She was afraid of things that might happen. This fear was so real to her that it affected every aspect of her life: her parenting, her leisure time, her marriage, her friendships, her lifestyle choices. She could gain some control over her fear with the use of prescription drugs, which she came to depend on. She added to her fear a terrible sense of guilt and failure that she, a Christian, could not control her life. She knew all the words about surrender and security in the Lord. She wanted desperately to find the peace she knew could . only be found in God. But she was afraid of God; afraid that if she surrendered to Him, He would test her by letting one of her fears come true.

It was a vicious cycle. But Chris never gave up. She turned to God over and over again in fear, failure, and desperation. Until she was 34 years old, nothing changed, at least not for long. Then, during a true crisis, when she seemed about to lose every material thing through no fault of her own, she found peace. Over a period of a few days, the light began to dawn. In one monumental act of surrender, empowered and directed by the Holy Spirit, Chris died to her old fears and embarked on a brand-new life. She is a completely changed person.

Her prayer life, her entire approach to God, is transformed. She faced the possibility of bankruptcy and personal humiliation because of a lawsuit against her husband. When I spoke to her before her surrender, she used phrases such as, "I'm just begging God . . . ," "I pray over and over again that God will . . ." She was emotionally distraught. She wanted assurances from me that God would act exactly as she had prescribed that He should. She thought peace would come when she knew for sure God would spare her and her family as she had dictated that He should. Later, her whole demeanor changed. She exuded peace and confidence. She told me: "For a while I continued to pray that God would do specific things, but I knew that if He chose to do something else, it was because He had a better plan. Now I don't even feel compelled to pray anything except 'Thy kingdom come, Thy will be done.' I am flooded with a sense of security in God, whatever the outcome." While circumstances pummel her, she is serene and confident. She is praying in the Spirit. (The lawsuit was resolved in her husband's favor. He was completely exonerated. Throughout the long ordeal and the days of the trial, Chris was supernaturally sustained by the indwelling Holy Spirit in a way she had never before experienced.)

I wrote this story about Chris more than 15 years ago. Since then, she has grown stronger and more stable. Of course, there were ups and downs along the way. There were times early in her transformation when she almost fell back into the old fears. But today she is one of the most peaceful people I know.

My friend Sara was the most insecure person I had ever met. She had been sexually abused as a child and was wary of everyone. She felt so worthless that she expected rejection. She interpreted every comment and every action as a personal affront. She was so shy that she would not initiate conversation even with people she had known for years. She had locked herself away in a prison from which no one could release her. When she accepted Christ as her Savior, her perspective began to change. She began to step out in faith and take risks by reaching out to people. However, she was still crippled by a ravaged self-esteem that kept her from reaching her potential. The steps she took toward wholeness were small and wobbly.

After about a year as a Christian, she experienced a deep longing to be filled more completely with the power of God. She asked God to fill her with His Spirit. She reports that she did not feel anything in particular. There was no overwhelming emotion or ecstatic experience. She simply trusted God to fulfill His Word. Over the next year, I saw great changes in her. She took more risks. She stopped taking things personally. She reached out to others in need. She is still journeying toward wholeness, as we all are. But she is a new person. Her prayer life has changed from one of fear and self-centeredness to one of powerful intercession. She continually reports the mighty works of God in the lives of those for whom she prays. She is praying in the Spirit.

I saw her recently when I was in her city. Seventeen years had passed since she surrendered more fully to the Holy Spirit. The old Sara was gone. A new Sara had taken her place. Her countenance was changed; her manner was changed.

These are only a few examples. I could tell you many stories of people transformed when they reached a moment of total surrender. However, being filled with the Spirit is not a one-time experience. The initial filling is maintained by continuous fillings. Once you are filled with the Spirit, you are to walk in the Spirit. The Spirit will direct your prayers according to the will of God. The Spirit will teach you to pray. The Spirit will reveal Christ within you.

Praying in the Spirit

Being filled with the Spirit will rearrange your prayer life. When the Spirit of God fills you, floods you, saturates you, you are totally reoriented. Self is dethroned and Christ enthroned. You are no longer the center of your existence, nor the center of your prayers. The Spirit of God reconstructs you so that you have a new set of desires, a new motivational center, and a new perspective. This happens immediately at the moment that God fills you with His Spirit, but is worked out over time in your experience. As you continue to yield to the Spirit and allow Him to fill you, you notice the new you emerging. Nowhere will your newness be more apparent than in your prayer life.

Jesus, in His discourse with the Samaritan woman by Jacob's well, told her, "'God is spirit, and his worshipers must worship in spirit and in truth" (John 4:24). Your relationship with God is to be on the deepest level. Prayer comes from your spirit and is based on the truth. The danger of religious formalities is that they may replace spiritual worship. This happened to the religious leaders of Jesus's day. They knew every detail of the ceremonial forms of worship, but when the intended object of their worship stood before them, they did not recognize Him. They had become so intent on the methods that they missed the truth.

We encounter the same danger today. We can go to our meetings, sing our hymns, perform our religious obligations, voice the acceptable opinions, do some good deeds, and never worship. Outward forms of worship were intended to express true, inward worship. The danger is that they will disguise inward emptiness.

The Holy Spirit is the guard against empty, surface religion. "But when He, the Spirit of truth, comes, He will guide you into all truth. He will not speak on his own; he will speak only what he hears, and he will tell you what is yet to come. He will bring glory to me by taking from what is mine and making it known to you" (John 16:13–14). The Holy Spirit is the Spirit of truth. He discloses Jesus who is Truth (John 14:6). The Father is seeking those who will worship Him in truth (John 4:23). The Holy Spirit is the power of God at work within you. He is the life of Christ flowing through you. He will lead you into all truth.

Having been filled with the Holy Spirit, you will be able to distinguish truth from illusion. Your judgment will not be limited to what your eye sees and what your ear hears. You will have a discernment that goes beyond facts and reason. Your mind will ascertain facts, but the Holy Spirit will disclose truth. Your praying will be based on revealed truth, not on opinion or emotion. The Spirit will glorify Christ within you so that your prayers are expressions of His desires.

For example, suppose there is a person in your life who is offensive and obnoxious to you. She is outspoken and tactless. She has hurt your feelings or irritated you more times than you can count. Every time she does, you self-righteously claim to forgive her. You think she is a burden you have to bear. Each time she offends you, you mentally inventory all her previous offenses. Because you are to pray for your enemies, you may even say prayers for her. You are well aware of the facts. The facts are that she is self-centered, thoughtless, demanding, and unkind. The facts shape your attitude toward her and your prayers for her.

What is the truth? When the Holy Spirit discloses the truth, your attitude changes and your prayers change. When, through the Spirit, you see the needs that dictate her actions, you see her in a new light. Now you can pray in truth. The same situations will occur. Before you allowed the Holy Spirit to fill you, you would have been angry, offended, and hurt. Now the same situation calls you to prayer and stirs up love. Now you don't think of her with anger, but with compassion. The Holy Spirit pours God's love into your heart and you share His attitude toward her. Now you are praying in the Spirit.

When you begin to worship God in spirit and in truth, the outward forms of religion become an extension and expression of your prayer life. You can't hide behind a life filled with church meetings and plastered with religious slogans. The Spirit of truth will lead you out of the land of your safe, comfortable existence into the needs and hurts of people. You will not be able to pray in the Spirit and be isolated from a dying world. However, you will confront these needs through the leading of the Spirit. You will be involved in Spirit-appointed tasks. These are tasks assigned in prayer and carried out through prayer. You will experience the joy of the Spirit as you are allowed to participate in establishing the kingdom of God in the hearts of people.

Praying Earnestly in the Spirit

Paul wrote to the Colossians that Epaphras was "'always wrestling in prayer for you, that you may stand firm in all the will of God, mature and fully assured" (Colossians 4:12). As an example of the effective prayer of a righteous person, James says that Elijah prayed earnestly. To pray earnestly means to pray passionately, with heart-felt emotion. Mechanical, dutiful praying is not praying in the Spirit.

Fervency, or earnestness, in prayer is not something you can work up. Spirit-born emotion is not fleeting or inconsistent. When you are praying in the Spirit, you will be praying with the fervency imparted to you by God. God, through His Spirit, will be reproducing His very own love and concern. The Holy Spirit prays through your spirit with emotions too deep to be expressed in words. You verbalize prayer as best you can, but the depths of God's feelings go far beyond what can be expressed in words.

"We do not know what we ought to pray for, but the Spirit

himself intercedes for us with groans that words cannot express. And he who searches our hearts knows the mind of the Spirit, because the Spirit intercedes for the saints in accordance with God's will" (Romans 8:26–27).

The Holy Spirit makes up for your limitations by continuing His intercession from His dwelling place, your spirit, in emotions too deep for words. Fervency will be inherent in Spirit-filled prayer. God will impart His emotions. You simply make yourself available to Him by surrendering to His Spirit within you.

Be Alert to the Spirit

Paul writes to the Colossians, "Devote yourselves to prayer, being watchful" (Colossians 4:2). In order to pray in the Spirit, you must be alert to the Spirit's guidance. The Holy Spirit does not come and go. He has taken up permanent residence within you. He flows through you as blood flows through your veins, imparting and maintaining life in your spirit. He is working in you continually.

There are two ways that the Holy Spirit's work can be hindered. He can be quenched (1 Thessalonians 5:19) and He can be grieved (Ephesians 4:30).

The word *quench* means to "extinguish," the same word used for "putting out a fire." The Holy Spirit is God who revealed Himself as fire again and again. He appeared in a burning bush to Moses. He led the children of Israel through the darkness of the wilderness as a fire. The eternal Shekinah (presence) of God existed as fire over the mercy seat. At Pentecost, that Fire invaded individuals, symbolized by tongues of fire that appeared over their heads. The same fire that once burned in the Most Holy Place now burns within us. That fire produces the fervency, the drive, the intensity of the Spirit-filled life. There are several things I have found that quench the Spirit in my life.

If I go for a period of time without practicing the spiritual disciplines, especially a daily extended prayertime, the fire of the Holy Spirit begins to fade. If I am deliberately disobedient, if I refuse to step out in faith at His leading, His fire fades. If I fill up my life with noises, like television and music, I lose the experience of His fire. I do not lose the Holy Spirit, but I am not allowing Him full access to my life. I am not alert to Him. I miss out on the intimacy and power He wants me to have.

To grieve the Holy Spirit means to make Him sorrowful. I'm not sure there is a distinct difference between grieving and quenching the Holy Spirit. I believe that they overlap. However, Paul's instruction not to grieve the Spirit is in a passage about behavior toward others. This passage warns against unwholesome language, bitterness and anger, quarreling, slandering, and such. (See Ephesians 4:25–32.) I can cause the Spirit sorrow by the way I represent Him to others. If I act just like my non-Christian friends by entering into unwholesome conversation, the Holy Spirit is grieved. If I gossip about someone or fail to treat someone with respect and love, I grieve the Holy Spirit. When I do these things, I feel His sorrow. He imparts His emotions to me and I feel grieved too.

When you have acted in a way that quenches or grieves the Holy Spirit, you have tied a tourniquet around your spiritual life. The life of Christ cannot flow through you, cleansing and empowering you. You cannot walk in the Spirit.

You need to confess and repent, receive God's forgiveness and cleansing, and take whatever steps are necessary to change your behavior and make amends. The Holy Spirit will immediately fill you again. You don't have to earn your way back into His favor.

To pray in the Spirit means to pray Spirit-directed prayers. You must be alert to the Spirit's still, small voice. Your attention must be centered on Him. Your spiritual senses must be actively attuned to His voice. You must open your life to His truth. You must ask Him to fill you and to keep on filling you. You will learn not to depend on your own understanding, but to be the vehicle through which the Holy Spirit expresses the thoughts of God.

C. H. Spurgeon, in *Classic Sermons on Prayer*, says, "For such prayer the work of the Holy Ghost Himself is needed. If prayer were of the lips alone, we should only need breath in our nostrils to pray. If prayer were of the desires alone, many excellent desires are easily felt, even by natural men. But when it is the spiritual desire, and the spiritual fellowship of the human spirit with the Great Spirit, then the Holy Ghost Himself must be present all through it to help infirmity and give life and power, or else true prayer will never be presented. The thing offered to God will wear the name and have the form, but the inner life of prayer will be far from it."

Meditation

Father, I feel that I am on the fringes of Your kingdom. I have touched the hem of Your garment, but have not looked into Your face. I believe in You, but I sense no power in prayer. There is a gnawing hunger in my soul.

My child, the work I will do is eternal. I do not respond to your demands. I respond to your heart's cry. I will satisfy that hunger in your soul. I will fill your emptiness. Feast at My table.

"'I am the bread of life. He who comes to me will never go hungry'" (John 6:35).

Reflection

1. Do you feel that you are filled with the Holy Spirit? If not, will you take the following steps?

   a. You must first have a deep hunger for God. If you do not, ask God to create that hunger within you.

   b. If you do feel that longing, ask God to show you what you need to relinquish in order to fully surrender to Him. Ask Him to make you willing and able.

   c. Ask God to fill you with His Spirit. Keep in mind that it is God who will do the work. You are His vessel. Trust God to do what He has been longing to do.

   d. Don't give yourself a schedule to follow. This whole process may take a few moments or a few months. God may need time to do major soul-surgery to remove deeply imbedded hindrances to Him. Trust Him to begin and to complete the process.

e. Walk in the Spirit.

2. Are you quenching or grieving the Holy Spirit? Will you repent and begin again to live in the fullness of the Spirit?

Review

1. What does it mean to be filled with the Spirit?

2. What does it mean to pray in the Spirit?

We have started a prayer triplet ministry where groups of three (or in some cases five) meet once a month for one hour to pray evangelistically for our church, our families, our country, and our government. We plan special prayer celebrations where we get together and share answers that each group has seen since our last gathering and pray corporately as well as worship in praise singing. It's wonderful! We have about 24 women. I've seen God heal deep and long-held-in wounds of people through these groups as they pray for their children and family members. I've seen women strengthened and increase in their desire to study the Word and to reach out to others in meaningful ministry.

Lucretia Mobbs
Helena, Alabama

Chapter 6

In Everything Give Thanks

"Always giving thanks to God the Father for everything in the name of our Lord Jesus Christ" (Ephesians 5:20).

"Give thanks in all circumstances, for this is God's will for you in Christ Jesus" (1 Thessalonians 5:18).

"Do not be anxious about anything, but in everything by prayer and petition with thanksgiving, present your requests to God" (Philippians 4:6).

Thanksgiving is an indispensable element of prayer. Notice how inclusive these exhortations are to thanksgiving. Always giving thanks, in everything give thanks, in everything pray with thanksgiving. Many people argue that this is an unrealistic or impractical requirement. Some feel that giving thanks in all circumstances is an escape from reality, a refusal to face and deal with the truth. If not properly understood, all these negatives can be true.

Praise and thanksgiving according to formula do not suffice. Praise and thanksgiving with an aim to manipulate God or as an instant cure for all problems will disappoint. Praise and thanksgiving as a substitute for reality, to cover over real feelings, is not true prayer. God calls you to thanksgiving grounded in reality and truth. He calls you to go beyond giving thanks; He calls you to be thankful. As in everything, He calls you to act out what you are, not act like what you're not. He does not want formalized thanksgiving that does not spring from a thankful heart. Once again, with your surrender, He will undertake to form His heart of thanksgiving within you.

Scripture is to be the springboard for your thanksgiving. Through Scripture, spoken into your understanding by the Holy Spirit, God reveals the basis for a thankful heart. Your thanksgiving is to be based on the nature and eternal purposes of God. The mind, heart, and life of God within you continually works to align your purposes with His. He is enlightening the eyes of your heart so that you will know the hope of His calling. (See Ephesians 1:18.) When you know the truth, thanksgiving and praise will flow spontaneously.

Be Thankful for Every Good Gift

"Every good and perfect gift is from above, coming down from the Father of the heavenly lights, who does not change like shifting shadows" (James 1:17). It seems obvious to thank God for the good things He brings to life. This is the most elementary lesson in the school of prayer. Yet, we don't do it very well. Two stumbling blocks occasionally enter my life and dilute my spontaneous, continuous giving of thanks for God's good gifts. First, I delight in the gift and exclude the Giver. Of course, I'm well trained and would rarely neglect to say thank you to God at some point. But my delight is in the gift. I forget that God's supply is meant to point me to Him, the Source. He delivers because He is the Deliverer. He blesses because He is the Blesser. He provides because He is the Provider. He rescues because He is the Rescuer. He is revealed in everything He does. His good things and perfect gifts are signposts pointing to Him. "'I have loved you with an everlasting love; I have drawn you with loving-kindness'" (Jeremiah 31:3).

When I allow God's goodness to point me to Him, I take nothing for granted. Everything in my life is a reason for thanksgiving. The sun came up this morning. It comes up every morning and has come up every morning since time began. The fact that this has occurred for centuries without fail does not lessen its impact. The first morning light always points my attention to the Father of lights, the Creator of the universe, without whom this reliable miracle would never have occurred. I don't mean that every morning I form the words, "Thank You for the sun." It has become an instinctual response that the sight of His creation points me to Him. He has built it in me. Everything points me to God, the source of every good gift. By building in me a thankful heart, He sensitizes me to His constant presence. By training yourself to acknowledge the good things that are so freely and so reliably given to you, you are keeping Him in view. When I fill my days with praise and thanksgiving, the problems and crises that come along are dwarfed by my awareness of His loving-kindness.

The second barrier to a thankful heart is that sometimes I look at my life from a one-dimensional perspective, and I see hurdles and disappointments galore. I don't have enough time to myself. I don't have enough money. I don't get enough attention. My house doesn't have enough room. Not enough of this and not enough of that. Soon, all the good and perfect gifts with which my life is filled are lost in the jumble of dissatisfactions. If I let it go on long enough, I can infect my whole family. I can poison the atmosphere of our home. I can have everyone dancing to my tune. My prayer life can become pitiful whining and feeling sorry for myself. I can demand to know why God would choose to burden me so. "If I have sinned, what have I done to you, O watcher of men? Why have you made me your target? Have I become a burden to you?" (Job 7:20).

When I am in this thankless state of mind, my whole life, especially my prayer life, is out of sync. My spirit is clothed in garments that don't fit. I am to be wearing "a garment of praise instead of a spirit of despair" (Isaiah 61:3). My outward expression does not reflect the Holy Spirit's work within me. God calls me back to Him, reminding me: "'My people will be filled with my bounty,' declares the Lord" (Jeremiah 31:14). There is no such thing as "enough" except in Him. The eyes of man are never satisfied. (See Proverbs 27:20.) Any time I seek satisfaction outside Him, I will be left empty. If I respond in obedience and begin to thank and praise Him, I find that "he satisfies the thirsty and fills the hungry with good things" (Psalm 107:9).

Praise and thanksgiving do not magically change my circumstances. They radically alter my viewpoint. Praise and thanksgiving bring me back into the presence of God, where there is fullness of joy and pleasures evermore. When you stare fixedly at a certain object, that object becomes magnified in your consciousness and surrounding objects fade in importance. This is a built-in function of your brain. The object of your attention is called your fixation point. This brain function is used to induce hypnosis, a state of consciousness in which one's mental focus is narrowed.

This brain function is a picture of how your spiritual eyes work. Wherever your gaze is fixed will be prominent in your thinking. You can fix your gaze on earth, or you can fix your gaze on Him. This will determine your perspective. If your fixation point is God, He will be magnified in your thinking. The impact of peripheral circumstances will diminish. "I will praise God's name in song and glorify him with thanksgiving" (Psalm 69:30).

For Paul, thoughts of friends and loved ones triggered praise. "I thank my God every time I remember you" (Philippians 1:3). "I always thank God for you" (1 Corinthians 1:4). The joy he felt in the people that he loved pointed him directly to God, the source of every good gift. The Holy Spirit can train you to let people ignite praise. Every time I think of the people I love, friends and family, I thank God for how He has used them to enrich my life. The pictures on my refrigerator of my children and my nieces call me to thanksgiving. As I address Christmas cards I am called to thanksgiving for each person on my list. These spontaneous eruptions of praise are not long and eloquent. Just quick expressions of gratitude.

One key to a thankful heart is to be mindful that *every* good thing is from God. While He may use a human vehicle to make delivery, He is the source of everything. The things you take for granted could become triggers for praise in His hands. Even the things that annoy you could be calls to thanksgiving. For example, paying bills may not be fun, but if you fix your gaze on Him, it could be a time of thanksgiving. "Thank You for the opportunity to have electricity in my home. . . . Thank You for the running water that makes my life so much easier. . . . Thank You for the roof over my head."

"Devote yourselves to prayer, being watchful and thankful" (Colossians 4:2). Always be alert to the Holy Spirit's leadership in prayer. Through Him, be alert to the blessings of God that call you to thanksgiving.

Be Thankful in the Midst of Difficulties

"Consider it pure joy, my brothers, whenever you face trials of many kinds" (James 1:2). Scripture teaches us that we are to welcome life's difficulties, consider them friends, count them as a joy. What a strange perspective. It makes sense to thank God for the good things, but thanking Him for the bad is another matter. Praise and thanksgiving in the difficulties of life must be deeply rooted in God's truth.

Thanksgiving in life's trials is built on a foundation of truth about God. First, God watches over you protectively and gives you His undivided attention. Nothing about you escapes His eye. He never looks away. I remember when my first son was born. I was so fascinated, so in awe of this little life I'd carried, that he was the focus of my days. I watched every move, listened to every sound. I memorized him. Every move he made, every emotion he felt, everything about his physical appearance was important to me. To me, it was as if he were the only baby ever born. This is how God sees you. God is not limited as are humans. Each of His children gets the same focused, undivided attention. His watchful care never leaves you. You are the most important thing in the world to Him. Nothing comes into your life without His permission. Every circumstance has been screened by Him before it touches you.

God knows you. He put you together in your mother's womb. He planned you. He knows how many hairs are on your head. Nothing about you is hidden from Him. You are His creation, His workmanship. He knows your needs, your potential, and your purpose. He knows what will bring you an eternal weight of glory. He knows how to tap your potential and bring you to spiritual maturity. No difficulty will come into your life unless it can be used by God for your benefit. When unpleasant circumstances occur, you can be assured that they have been evaluated by God, and He has determined that the eternal glory they will produce far outweighs the momentary affliction.

"Before I was afflicted I went astray, but now I obey your word, ... It was good for me to be afflicted so that I might learn your decrees. The law from your mouth is more precious to me than thousands of pieces of silver and gold" (Psalm 119:67, 71–72).

A thankful heart requires an eternal perspective. If your goals are short-term and material, the difficulties you encounter will be stumbling blocks. If, however, your goal is to be made in the likeness of Christ, life's difficulties will be stepping-stones. God will use the circumstances that could tear you down to build you up. He will not bless you in spite of the circumstances, but by means of them. "I will turn all my mountains into roads" (Isaiah 49:11).

Based on these two truths, you can begin to thank God for every circumstance. You are not thanking Him because you enjoy the circumstances. You are not expressing delight in the difficulty, but delight in God, whose purpose is unchanging, whose power is unlimited, whose love is eternal. You don't have to understand how each circumstance will be used for your benefit. God invites us to draw near in the full assurance of faith, even when there is no understanding. As you have been walking with God, filled with His Spirit, with Christ's life flowing through you, difficulties will look different to you. The ability to thank God for trials is part of the whole prayer package, set in the context of your walk with Him. You do not suddenly develop an eternal perspective when faced with hardship. A thankful heart is one of the benefits of living beyond the veil, in the very presence of God.

Let me illustrate through the experience of the late Hugh Wamble, professor of church history, Midwestern Baptist Theological Seminary. Hugh spent the past 40-plus years following God's call in ministry. As he neared retirement, he was diagnosed with a malignant brain tumor. Left alone in the office of the diagnostic radiologist, just having heard the heartbreaking news, Hugh immediately began to review the previous months. He clearly saw God's hand preparing him for this moment.

"I began to praise God for His providential care evidenced in the twists and turnings of circumstances during the preceding weeks and months." He told his neurosurgeon: "God has directed my steps all along the way. He has placed me in your care. I have great confidence in what you will do." Hugh's prayer life during his trial gives evidence of the Holy Spirit's long and thorough work. "I prayed that day that God would protect me against the temptation to be selfish in my praying and self-centered in my living. I asked Him not to allow me to corrupt this meaningful experience with a self-centered attitude. Although my future was uncertain, He knew and would oversee what happened. I recommitted myself to Him to continue in my ministry to the extent that He gave me time and opportunity. On that day I came to a new agreement with God. He gave me assurance that some of my best ministry is yet to be.

"I asked God to daily give me the ability to live so that anyone who had contact with me would feel better at the end of the conversation than when the contact began. I want my life to certify or prove the authenticity of my relationship with God. I pray that God will cultivate in me the virtue of gratitude, realizing that self-pity and gratitude cannot flourish in the same soul. God has wonderfully blessed these prayers."

Hugh Wamble's heart was indisputable proof of God indwelling man through the Holy Spirit. God could heal Hugh suddenly and miraculously; or He could use medicine to heal Hugh, despite the medical opinions to the contrary; or He could let the disease run its course and usher Hugh into eternity. The proof of God's care is not in how He planned to use Hugh's disease. The proof of God's care is in the praise and thanksgiving of Hugh. (Dr. Wamble was killed in a car accident on September 22, 1991. God took him before he ever felt the ravages of his disease. He leaves behind a rich legacy.)

I had learned the power of thanksgiving through the course of many circumstances, but the death of my husband made all the others seem miniscule. The Lord reminded me daily, and reminds me daily still, that He holds my husband, my sons, and me in His hands and that He is working out everything towards an end that is good, pleasing, and perfect.

Let me share with you some of my journal entries from the darkest hours.

When negative, self-pitying, fearful thoughts knock on the door of my mind and seek admittance, I have a plan.

I can't wish them away, or stick my fingers in my ears, or deny that they are there. That won't work. Instead, I will use a spiritual chemotherapy against them. I will target them for destruction by directing the power of praise right at the core of them. I have formulated an aggressive, overpowering spiritual cocktail of truth, praise, peace, and thanksgiving.

"Bless the *Lord*, O my soul;
And all that is within me, bless His holy name!
Bless the *Lord*, O my soul,
And forget not all His benefits:
Who forgives all your iniquities,
Who heals all your diseases,
Who redeems your life from destruction,
Who crowns you with lovingkindness and tender mercies,
Who satisfies your mouth with good things,
So that your youth is renewed like the eagle's"
(Psalm 103:1–5).

I am crowned with tender mercies . . . such as:

For 26 years I have had a life partner who encourages me to follow my vision, and who rejoices with me in my successes and spurs me on in my disappointments. I have never had to hold myself back or deny my abilities in order to protect a fragile ego. Because of Wayne, I could be fully me.

We have three grown sons whose character is formed and solid. We are comforted to know that they are strong and that their faith is real.

We see daily the provision made for us before we knew that we would need it. For example, our middle son, Kennedy, a recent Baylor graduate, had planned several months ago to move home for a while and save on expenses while he pursues some opportunities. He arrived home on the night before we received Wayne's diagnosis. We have Kennedy at home to help us just when we need him.

We have a lifetime collection of friends to stand beside us. We have extended families who give us strength and support. I have a career that leaves me in charge of my own schedule.

I had an office away from home for 15 years, but after our youngest left for college, I moved my office home. How much easier that makes these coming days!

I have an assistant, Terry Trieu, who is the most competent and responsible person on earth and whom I can count on completely. She knows how to run my daily business better than I do!

We are, indeed, crowned with tender mercies, of which this list is but a shadow.

Be Thankful in Difficulties in the Lives of Loved Ones

It is easier to suffer yourself than to watch someone you love suffer. It may be easier to thank God for your own difficulties than to thank Him for the hardships of those you love. In our earthbound love, we so want to spare our loved ones any pain. God brought this to my attention as I prayed for my sister to have the child she longed for. For 10 years, Julie wanted a baby. As the months and years dragged on, piling disappointment on disappointment, my heart broke with her. My prayers were constantly beseeching God to give her a baby.

One morning God brought it to my attention that my prayers for her were very different from my prayers for my own difficulties. God had taught me to thank Him in every circumstance in my life, good or bad. He had shown me over and over how everything works together for good. I was so intent on sparing Julie pain that I was not thanking God for her circumstance, knowing that He already had the answer prepared, the timing planned, and that He was at work in her life redemptively. I was not willing to let her walk through trials to become all that God intended.

That morning I began to thank God for every day of her wait. I thanked God for the baby that would be born. I thanked Him for the spiritual strength He was building in her. I thanked God for His timing. It was still several years before her daughter, Hannah Catherine, came along. I don't think that my thanksgiving hurried God's plan. It allowed me to cooperate with God through intercession, instead of work against Him. It changed my outlook and released me to pray in the Spirit instead of in my own wisdom.

My friend Jan (not her real name) discovered that her young child had been sexually abused. She was shattered. She felt excruciating pain for her child, rage toward the perpetrator, frustration at the legal system, and disappointment with God. How could she possibly thank God for this? She felt that she could thank God if something so terrible had happened to her, but she felt it almost a betrayal of her child to thank God for this. Through those first dark days, her prayers could not go past asking God how He could have let this happen. Where was He? Little by little, God helped her begin to work through her anger with Him and led her to a deeper understanding of Him. Then she began to take little steps toward forgiving her enemies. She saw her child respond to Christian counseling and display a spiritual wisdom that could only be a gift from God.

One morning God told her, "It's time now to start thanking Me." Here she balked. The Holy Spirit continued to nudge her until she began to thank Him based on what she knew about Him, even though the circumstances did not seem to prove the truth.

One day shortly after, she was in a small Bible study group. The Holy Spirit seemed to prompt her to share her experience. She felt that she could not. The pain was too raw, and she still had so far to go toward inner healing. It was not something she wanted to tell. Finally, the Holy Spirit said, "You must tell your experience or My purpose here will not be accomplished." So she tearfully told her story. (These women did not know her child or live in the same city, and she did not identify the child by name.)

As she finished, several of the women were in tears. As it turned out, nearly every woman there had experienced sexual abuse in their own lives or in the life of a child and in every case it was a barrier to prayer. Her obedience allowed God's light to shine into some very dark corners. A great inner healing began that day. For the first time, she could say with her mouth and with her heart, thank You. She saw that God would use even this for good.

Several years have now passed. She can now thank God for how He has used her child's terrible experience. She can see how it has created a strong bond in their family and a level of trust among family members. God has performed a miracle in using this experience to build a young person of deep compassion and a sense of God's mercy. He has turned a mountain into a road.

As I walk my grief journey, I can tell you that the hardest part of all is that I can't spare my sons their grief. I have to just let them hurt. Each time I remember their pain, it is an act of my will that only the Holy Spirit can generate to thank God for what He is doing in them. Yet I know—I know—that God is developing in them character and faith and compassion and love that will enrich their lives. I know that God is teaching them what a Father He wants to be to them. I know that He is adding value to their lives that could not have come any other way. And I thank Him for that.

When God creates a thankful heart, true praise and thanksgiving flow in every circumstance, yours or your loved ones'. When your goals for yourself and for those you love are eternal, every experience is permitted by God in order to move you toward the goal of Christlikeness.

Make Your Requests with Thanksgiving

"Do not be anxious about anything, but in everything, by prayer and petition with thanksgiving, present your requests to God. And the peace of God, which transcends all understanding, will guard your hearts and your minds in Christ Jesus" (Philippians 4:6–7). God wants you to let your needs and desires be known to Him. He tells you not to have anxiety about anything, but instead to pray about everything. The secret, He says, is to bring your requests to Him with thanksgiving. You can thank Him in advance because you are acquainted by experience with His character and His ways.

God tells you to tell Him your needs and desires and thank Him at the same time. Sometimes the thanksgiving that accompanies petition is based on what you know about God. In other words, you may present a need not knowing how He will meet it, but certain that He will. Thank God that you have that need because it pulls you to Him. Thank God that He cares about that need and has the answer prepared. Thank Him that He will meet that need according to His wisdom and for your benefit. Thank God that as you wait on Him to have that need met, He will satisfy you with Himself.

Sometimes God will give you assurance and an inner certainty of how a need will be met or desire fulfilled. You probably will not know the timing or the method, but you know the outcome. You can thank God specifically in advance for the answer He has already given in your spirit. The reality in your spirit is truth, the substance of things hoped for, the evidence of things not seen.

The petition aspect of your prayer life should be wrapped in praise and thanksgiving. When it is, the peace of God, beyond comprehension, guards your mind and heart from anxiety.

Meditation

Weed out bitterness. Let praise take root and flourish. Cultivate my life so that it will display Your beauty. Make my life like a watered garden, lush with the Spirit's fruit.

"You will be like a well-watered garden" (Isaiah 58:11).

Reflection

1. List the good gifts God has placed in your life. Thank Him for each one. Ask the Holy Spirit to make you aware of every good gift every day.

2. List the difficulties you are facing. Thank God for each one. Meditate on the mercy and power of God which He will display through your problems.

Review

1. On what basis are you to give thanks in all circumstances?

2. What can diminish your ability to give thanks?

Heart's Cry

Chapter 7

Stand in the Gap

"'I looked for a man among them who would build up the wall and stand before me in the gap on behalf of the land'" (Ezekiel 22:30).

"So he said he would destroy them, had not Moses, his chosen one, stood in the breach before him to keep his wrath from destroying them" (Psalm 106:23).

God has declared that He will be like a refiner and smelter of silver. As we discussed in chapter 3, one property of silver is that it conducts light and electricity. Electricity is transmitted to its destination through a conductor, a substance through which power freely moves. The conductor transmits power from the source to the need.

Intercessors are God's conductors. Whatever God wants to pour into the world, He will pour through intercessors. Jesus' outline for intercession is: "'Thy kingdom come, Thy will be done on earth as it is in heaven'" (Matthew 6:10). He points out the gap between heaven and earth. To paraphrase, His intercession is, "Let your will be done on earth the same way it is done in heaven. I stand before You as the conductor of Your will into the circumstances of earth." A divine transfer takes place. In the unseen, spiritual world, God's will begins to flow to earth through your prayers.

Intercession Assigned by God

You cannot be an intense intercessor for every need. Every time you hear of a need or have contact with a person, you can spontaneously intercede. I have learned to pray silently, "Let Your kingdom come. Let Your will be done." For prolonged, disciplined intercession, God must make the assignment. If you are available to Him, He will place a burden of intercession on you for particular people, countries, or situations. With time and practice, you will learn to recognize this burden and respond to it. When God does place this burden on you, it is a sure signal that He wants to do something and wants His power to flow through your prayers.

Norman and Beverly Coad, former missionaries to Mali, felt the need for intercessors who would pray specifically and daily for the evangelization of the West African country. The Coads had already enlisted intercessors for their own ministry since it began. "We recognized in a hurry that opening work in countries with centuries of Muslim influence had to have the anointing of the Lord or it would be a disaster," says Norman. "We felt very, very, very in over our heads—Little Leaguers playing in major-league games—so we asked people we knew or heard about who were really dedicated prayer warriors to lift up our ministry."

The Baptist Mission of Mali had an opportunity to expand their ministry into Kenieba, a remote rural area cut off from the rest of civilization by geography. The government invited Southern Baptists to work in Kenieba because it is so remote that other groups weren't interested.

As the ministry began, the missionaries decided to enlist a prayer warrior support group to intercede for the new ministry. They didn't know how to enlist the prayer supporters, so the missionaries prayed. "People none of us knew began to write," says Beverly Coad. "They'd say they had noticed our name in an article or on the prayer calendar and had been led to contact us and pledge to pray for our requests if we'd share them."

The missionaries began to keep a prayer log, listing prayer partners and specific prayer requests. Results are recorded. God had placed in the missionaries an awareness of their need for intercession. He called out the intercessors whom He had assigned. He is working through the intercessors to touch the lives of people they will probably never see. There are no boundaries on intercession.

Just as the subject of your intercession will be assigned by God, so will the content. You are conducting the will of God into the situation, not instructing God on how He should handle it. The starting point of intercession is to listen to Him. How we see a situation and how God sees it are often very different. We tend to see the outside edges of the need, He sees the core. While you may want to see a person rescued from a bad situation immediately, God's focus is probably the work He's doing through the situation. You must cooperate with God in establishing His will in the circumstance. If you are trying to wheedle Him into working faster, or taking an easier course, you are not interceding. God does not have to be convinced to love a person more, or have more compassion. He does not have to be nudged and reminded to come up with a solution. He had the answer prepared before He ever assigned you to intercede.

Bring your burden of intercession before Him and ask: *Father, how shall I intercede?* Remember, you are filled with the Holy Spirit. God reveals His thoughts to us through His Spirit. "God has revealed it to us by His Spirit. The Spirit searches all things, even the deep things of God" (1 Corinthians 2:10). Jesus said that the Holy Spirit will teach you all things, guide you into all truth, and make Christ known to you. (See John 14:25–26; 16:13–15.)

You know that it is always God's will that you thank Him. "Give thanks in all circumstances, for this is God's will for you in Christ Jesus" (1 Thessalonians 5:18). Open your intercession by thanking God for everything you can see to be thankful for. Then thank Him for the things that do not look like reasons to be thankful, based on the truth about God and His ways. Wait until the Holy Spirit begins to form a prayer in your heart. When you have asked God to guide you, you will need to trust your spiritual instincts, even when they clash with your mental assessment. When you are praying in the Spirit, there will be a sense of oneness with God, a harmony with the Spirit. You will come to know it.

Jesus is always interceding (Hebrews 7:25). The Holy Spirit is interceding through you (Romans 8:26). The Holy Spirit's role is to disclose Christ to you and to take what is Christ's and reveal it to you. Therefore, the Holy Spirit will reveal Christ's intercession in you. Jesus's intercession will be reproduced in you.

Let me give an illustration of this principle. My son, Kennedy, when he was little, had a method for presenting his petitions to his parents when he wasn't sure how they would be received. He told his little brother, Stinson, to ask for him. Kennedy would say, "Stinson, go ask Mom and Dad if we can do so-and-so." Kennedy's expressed desire ignited that same desire in his little brother. Stinson boldly brought Kennedy's desire, now also Stinson's desire, to my husband and me. "May Kennedy and I do so-and-so?" He expressed Kennedy's desire as if it were his own. Kennedy's desire had been exactly reproduced in his little brother. Stinson, in expressing his own desire, also expressed Kennedy's desire.

As all illustrations, this is inadequate. I am not implying that Jesus has the same motives as Kennedy. But can you see how one person's desire can be reproduced in another? Does this illustration help you understand how, when you are praying in the Spirit, your desires are really expressions of Jesus's desires? This is a crude representation of how the Holy Spirit reproduces Jesus's intercessory life in you.

Here's how this process works in your prayer life. I read this morning in Daniel 5:14: "I have heard that the spirit of the gods is in you and that you have insight, intelligence and outstanding wisdom." That sentence grabbed my attention. It ignited my desire for my sons to display the Spirit of God and to have insight, intelligence, and outstanding wisdom. This was the content of my intercession for them this morning. Jesus's desire, revealed in Scripture, ignited that very desire in me. When I presented my petition to the Father, I was expressing Jesus's intercession reproduced in me.

This is not an instant process. To be a powerful intercessor, a conductor of God's will, you must be willing to invest time. You must be willing for God to engrave that need on your heart where you will bear it before Him continually. (See Exodus 28:29–30.) The need for which you are interceding will become part of you. You must be willing to wait before God for His leading. God will lead you, if you are open to Him, by creating His desires in you so that they become your desires. Begin by praying, "Let Your kingdom come in this circumstance or this life. Let Your will be done on earth as it is in heaven." As you continue, God will fill in the outline of your prayer with more specifics.

Scripture Will Guide Your Intercession

The content of your intercession will be outlined in Scripture. Intercession flows from God's heart. Listen to God in His Word and He will shape your intercession. For example, during a time in my marriage when our relationship was strained, I was frustrated and felt unable to intercede. One morning God spoke this to me as I was reading in Jeremiah: "I will give [you and Wayne] singleness of heart and action, so that [you] will always fear me for [your] own good and the good of [your] children after [you]" (Jeremiah 32:39).

My spirit recognized God showing me His heart, His desire for my marriage. I knew this was how Jesus was interceding for my marriage. I began to join Him, and He reproduced His desire in me. I no longer had to try to convince myself that God would work. He told me so Himself. It was not long until God began to bring His Word to pass.

My friend Bobbie was worried about her daughter who was going through a period of rebellion in her young adult years. The Holy Spirit impressed this prayer on Bobbie from Isaiah 62: "For [Brooke's] sake I will not keep silent, for [Brooke's] sake I will not remain quiet [before God], till her righteousness shines out like the dawn, her salvation like a blazing torch. . . . [She] will be called by a new name that the mouth of the Lord will bestow. [She] will be a crown of splendor in the Lord's hand, and a royal diadem in the hand of your God" (Isaiah 62:1, 3). When God reveals His intentions through Scripture, we, as intercessors, know what to pray. We pray the will of God. The outcome is certain.

Recognizing God's voice through His Word requires being filled with the Spirit. He has to speak Scripture to your spiritual ears. He will make His Word personal and specific for you. You will have solid ground on which to base your faith.

Intercessors Must Identify with Need

As God gives you assignments for intercession, He will cause you to identify with the need. The need will feel like your own. Look at some examples of intercessors. Moses left the comforts of Egypt in order to identify with the people of God, for whom He became an ardent intercessor. (See Hebrews 11:25.) His identification with the people of Israel was so complete that He asked God to forgive their sin. "But now, please forgive their sin—but if not, then blot me out of the book you have written" (Exodus 32:32). He did not distinguish between his own good and theirs because God had engraved them on his heart and made them a part of him.

God assigned Daniel to intercede for his people to be freed from Babylonian captivity. God's desire was revealed to Daniel as he read from the book of the prophet Jeremiah. (See Daniel 9:2.) God instilled His own desire in Daniel so that Daniel began to seek God and intercede according to His revelation. Daniel identified with the sins of his people. "We have sinned . . . we have not listened . . . nor have we obeyed the voice of the Lord our God." (See Daniel 10.) Daniel was the link between the source and the need. He identified with the desires of God and with the needs of the people. He was not falsely confessing something he hadn't done. His people were so deeply engraved on his heart that he did not separate himself from them. He took their burdens on himself.

Jesus is the truest, greatest intercessor. In His role as eternal high priest, He brings us into the presence of God. Jesus is the link between you and God. He is the intercessor, the One who brings two parties together. The high priest of the Old Covenant made intercession for the people once a year (Hebrews 9:7). Many different men have held the office of high priest because as one died, another took his place (Hebrews 7:23). Jesus, in contrast, is the eternal high priest who abides in the presence of God, making continual and uninterrupted intercession. "But He, on the other hand, because He abides forever, holds His priesthood permanently. Hence, also, He is able to save forever those who draw near to God through Him, since He always lives to make intercession for them" (Hebrews 7:24–25).

Two things qualify Jesus to be our intercessor. One, He is completely identified with God and His desires. "Such a high priest meets our need—one who is holy, blameless, pure, set apart from sinners, exalted above the heavens" (Hebrews 7:26). Two, He is completely identified with us in our need. "For we do not have a high priest who is unable to sympathize with our weaknesses, but we have one who has been tempted in every way just as we are—yet was without sin" (Hebrews 4:15). He is able to link the need and the source.

One of Jesus's intercessory prayers for His disciples is recorded in John 17. First we see Jesus as the conductor of the will of God into the lives of His disciples: "that he might give eternal life to all those you have given him. Now this is eternal life: that they may know you. . . . I have brought you glory on earth. . . . I have revealed you to those whom you gave me out of the world. . . . For I gave them the words you gave me and they accepted them."

Next we see Jesus, the Son of man, calling on God, the source, to meet the needs of those with whom He is identified. He brings the need to the supply. "I will remain in the world no longer, but they are still in the world, and I am coming to you. Holy Father, protect them by the power of your name, the name you gave me—so that they may be one as we are one. . . . Protect them from the evil one. . . . Sanctify them by the truth." On the principle of "ask, and it shall be given you," every request that Jesus made according to the will of God released that very supply. As intercessors, our prayers release God's power and are the conduit through which His will comes to earth.

Richard Foster, in *Prayer: Finding the Heart's True Home,* says, "The true prophetic message always calls us to stretch our arms out wide and embrace the whole world. In holy boldness we cover the earth with the grace and mercy of God."

Intercessors May Be Participants in the Answers to Their Prayers

As you enter into a ministry of intercession, you must be willing to be used in answer to your prayers when called. The three intercessors listed above, Moses, Daniel, and Jesus, were all active in ministry as well as intercession. The two merged. Ministry was conceived in intercession and intercession grew out of ministry. Usually, or at least often, a burden of intercession is also a call to ministry. The ministry must be born of the Spirit, just like the intercession. The intercessor must wait before the Lord for wisdom in ministry. Otherwise you may rush to meet the outside edge of the need and miss the core. You can only be a conductor of the life of Christ when you are connected at the source.

As an intercessor, you are not always called on to participate physically in the answer. Sometimes God's command is, "Don't interfere. Don't rescue. Don't speak." This is especially hard when you have the resources that would bring a quick fix. God wants to teach you that His spiritual resources are adequate. He wants to teach you that you can tap His power through prayer alone, if He so decrees. The times that God has called on me to refrain from acting have been the times my faith was most challenged. Through those experiences I have learned about the power of God to move directly on hearts and minds to accomplish His purposes. I have seen God change people's minds far more effectively than my most persuasive argument could have accomplished.

God Will Not Be Hurried

There is much to be learned while waiting on God. His apparent delays are not delays. He is always working. "Jesus said to them, 'My Father is always at his work to this very day, and I, too, am working'" (John 5:17). He is always in the process of answering.

When Stinson was a little boy, he walked into the kitchen and said, "Mom, I'm ready for breakfast now." Before he asked me, I knew what I would fix for his breakfast. I had all the ingredients ready; however, I waited until he felt his need. Otherwise, he wouldn't eat the breakfast I prepared. When he asked for me to, I began to mix the ingredients into a coffee cake, preheat the oven, pour the ingredients into a pan, place the pan in the oven, and set the timer. Stinson returned in a few minutes, which seems like "ages" in a child's perception. "Mom, you said you'd fix my breakfast ages ago." I replied, "I did fix your breakfast. It's in the oven. When it's completely baked, I'll put it on the table for you to eat."

What looks like delay to the immature or uninformed, doesn't mean a request isn't being answered. When the answer is ready to be revealed, it will be. God calls for persevering prayer, which will be addressed in detail in the next chapter. If Stinson had stayed in the kitchen with me, he would not have hastened the process, but he would have seen the process. He would have had complete assurance that his breakfast was on the way. He would have been confident that the time for his breakfast to be set before him was settled.

Jesus taught that the kingdom of God works on the growth principle. There is always a process of revelation. In this process, there will be a period of no apparent progress. The Spirit-filled intercessor will recognize this as that stage of the process when the work of God is underground. Jesus tells this parable:

"This is what the kingdom of God is like. A man scatters seed on the ground. Night and day whether he sleeps or gets up, the seed sprouts and grows, though he does not know how. All by itself the soil produces grain—first the stalk, then the head, then the full kernel in the head. As soon as the grain is ripe, he puts the sickle to it, because the harvest has come" (Mark 4:26–29).

The farmer plants the seed and provides the needed care. He doesn't worry about how that little seed will turn into an ear of corn. He simply pulls up the weeds and does all the maintenance required to allow the seed to grow. Your persevering prayer is not to change God's course, or wear Him down, but to provide the spiritual maintenance while God works through the process.

God's creation is filled with illustrations of His working through the process. Think about the incubation period during which a bird's fertilized egg reaches maturity and hatches a baby bird. Once a bird lays her eggs, she sits on them to incubate them. To the uninformed observer, it would appear that nothing is happening. That observer would be amazed if he knew just how much was happening. The incubating bird has tucked her eggs underneath her stomach feathers close to a bare spot called her incubation patch. The incubation patch is the warmest surface on the bird's body because of the network of blood vessels that lie close to the surface and produce heat. This heat is readily passed from the mother bird to her eggs. Her waiting is deliberate. The delay is essential to the outcome. All the work is invisible to the physical eye. As the mother sits on her eggs, the embryo is growing to a fully formed chick. When the chick is ready, it will hatch.

Our persevering intercession provides the incubating heat needed for our Spirit-born desires to reach maturity.

Prayers for the salvation of Joash Obolla in Nairobi, Kenya, had a long incubation period. Elizabeth, Joash's wife, was saved and joined Parklands Baptist Church in Nairobi. She asked the church to pray for her husband. For more than a decade, Elizabeth and the church prayed for Joash. Six missionaries, Zeb and Evelyn Moss, James and Gena Hampton, and Dale and Beulah Hooper interceded faithfully and persistently. Over those ten years, when they may have been discouraged in their praying because they saw no results, God was at work. Step-by-step He was drawing Joash to Himself in response to persistent prayers.

Joash was consistently confronted with the witness of Christians. Even in his job as an immigration officer at Kenyetta International Airport, God was working. "It seemed like everyone who came past my desk knew me and knew I wasn't a Christian," says Joash. In 1989, a Bible study and prayer cell began meeting in the Obolla home. Joash began sitting in and attending church. Then his brother-in-law accepted Christ, and Joash attended his baptism. The next day he called missionary Charles Tope and that evening accepted Christ as his Savior.

Little by little, Joash's resistance had been worn away. The power of God continued to be poured into His life through intercessors. Joash came to Christ just like the seed grows into a plant—first the blade, then the head, then the mature grain.

God is looking for intercessors, those who will enter into His divine desires and cooperate with Him in establishing His kingdom on earth. God is calling for purified conductors of His life. He is calling you.

Meditation

Dear Intercessor: Think My thoughts. Empty yourself and become a servant. Bear on your heart the world's needs. Let go of your desires for toys and short-term delights. Embrace eternity; store up everlasting treasure. Enter into My joy.

"Your attitude should be the same as that of Christ Jesus, who . . . made Himself nothing, taking the very nature of a servant. . . . Therefore God exalted Him to the highest place" (Philippians 2:5, 7, 9).

Reflection

1. Are you willing to become a true intercessor?

2. If you are, ask God to burden you with the needs of others. Respond to the slightest sense of burden.

3. Stop and listen. What is God saying to you? Write it down.

Review

1. What is an intercessor?

2. How can you know how to pray according to God's will?

I belong to a group of lay women called BOWS (Blessing Our World Servants). We minister to missionaries on stateside assignment. Two of us meet with a local missionary to pray weekly for missionaries' emailed prayer requests. It connects me with them and the work God is accomplishing through their ministries around the world better than any other way because the needs are so fresh. I would not trade this for the world.
Judy Blakemore
Loveland, Colorado

Chapter 8

Ask . . . Seek . . . Knock

"Ask and it will be given to you; seek and you will find; knock and the door will be opened to you. For everyone who asks receives; he who seeks finds; and to him who knocks, the door will be opened" (Matthew 7:7–8).

"Give us today our daily bread" (Matthew 6:11).

God invites you to draw upon His resources for your daily needs—physical, emotional, or spiritual. God will provide for you in a practical way. He created your earthbound, time-bound frame and is prepared to meet your every need. God does not have a set of resources with fixed limits. His riches cannot be depleted if used too often. He pleads with you to come to Him in every circumstance, and to come again and again. He is never tired of hearing from you and providing for you. He rejoices over you and rejoices in doing good things for you. If something touches you, it touches Him. You are the apple of His eye. He dotes on you and longs to lavish His love and wealth on you. He wants you, by a choice of your free will, to turn to Him and accept all He wants to give. He waits for you to respond to His generosity by asking, seeking, and knocking.

Ask with Unpretentious Faith

Jesus said, "'I tell you the truth, unless you change and become like little children, you will never enter the kingdom of heaven'" (Matthew 18:3). To see the kingdom of God clearly, one must leave behind adult pretenses and sophisticated arguments. Often, we come to God prepared to do battle with Him, convince Him of the validity of our need and give Him reasons to meet it.

What a contrast to the way a little child comes to his or her parents. A child simply assumes that the need or desire is potent enough to speak for itself. All that is required is to bring that need to Mom's or Dad's attention. The request assumes the answer. The child's only thought is to bring the need to the source of supply.

You don't need to build a theological case for why God should want to meet your need. He wants to meet your need because He's your daddy and you are the apple of His eye. Jesus highlights the simplicity of supplication by saying, "Ask and it will be given to you. . . . For everyone who asks receives" (Matthew 7:7–8). The Greek word translated "ask" is used to ask for something to be given, not done. It is the simplest, most straightforward picture of asking for something you need.

Jesus elaborates on this principle further in the following verses.

"Which of you, if his son asks for bread, will give him a stone? Or if he asks for a fish, will give him a snake? If you, then, though you are evil, know how to give good gifts to your children, how much more will your Father in heaven give good gifts to those who ask him!" *(Matthew 7:9–11).*

The purest, most unselfish love I have is for my children. For them, I would lay down my life without thinking twice. Their needs are more important than my own. Without flinching, I would make any sacrifice for their happiness. A parent's love for his or her children, in the best of cases, most closely resembles God's love for us. To even begin to understand God's love for us, we would have to take the highest love we know and multiply it by infinity. If you would give good gifts to your children, how much more would God give to His? I don't have to be convinced to give my children what they need. I want to meet their needs. God "richly blesses all who call on him" (Romans 10:12).

Your asking should be anxiety free. "Do not worry about your life" (Matthew 6:25). Jesus tells you that God is aware of your material needs. You can simply ask for your daily needs to be met without having to remind God, and then focus your attention on the kingdom of God and His righteousness. God wants to free you from anxiety about your daily needs so that you will be able to focus on Him. (See Matthew 6:25–34.)

Seek with Determined Faith

Jesus invites you to seek and promises that you will find. For each word—*ask, seek, knock*—a linear tense is used. This means to ask and keep on asking; seek and keep on seeking; knock and keep on knocking. Seeking prayer is a lifelong quest.

Seeking prayer is different from asking prayer. In seeking prayer, you will be actively involved in a search. The Greek word for *seek* implies to seek something in order to find and possess it. It does not mean to seek in order to understand or to seek opportunity. What is it that you are to seek?

"But seek first his kingdom and his righteousness, and all these things will be given to you" (Matthew 6:33). Seek the kingdom of God in order to possess it. Everyone who seeks, finds.

The key to seeking prayer is to determine the focus of your search. Jesus tells you that the search for the kingdom of God and His righteousness is a guaranteed reward. This is not a search for divine blessing, or personal gain, or physical comfort. The seeking prayer is: *Father, I want to possess Your kingdom and Your righteousness. I don't want to just know about it. I want it to be mine. I will seek and keep on seeking until I possess every square inch of Your kingdom and every bit of Your righteousness.* Set your face like flint. Fix your eyes on your goal. The faith for seeking prayer says, *I will have it.* Seeking prayer requires determined faith.

Scripture is the map to guide your search. Jesus told many parables describing the kingdom of heaven. It cannot be summed up in a few words or paragraphs. In fact, the kingdom of heaven cannot be written down at all. At best, words and descriptions can point you in the right direction. "For the kingdom of God is not a matter of talk, but of power" (1 Corinthians 4:20).

As you begin your search, understand that it is God's great desire that you enter and possess His kingdom and His righteousness. "Do not be afraid, little flock, for your Father has been pleased to give you the kingdom" (Luke 12:32). He will not try to hide or disguise it. Seeking prayer will not take you through a labyrinth, but down a straight and narrow road. The way to the kingdom is a person. Jesus said, "I am the way" (John 14:6). The life of Christ flowing through you is the kingdom and righteousness.

The search for the kingdom of God is conducted through prayer. The kingdom is hidden from your physical senses and can only be revealed by the Holy Spirit. "'The kingdom of God does not come with your careful observation nor will people say, "Here it is," or "There it is," because the kingdom of God is within you'" (Luke 17:20–21). The kingdom is not experienced physically, but through the Holy Spirit. (See Romans 14:17.)

Seeking prayer brings this attitude to every situation. "Thy kingdom come. Thy will be done on earth as it is in heaven. In every situation, in every person, through every difficulty, establish Your kingdom. Use every situation, every person, every difficulty to give me more of the kingdom, to establish Your righteousness more deeply within me." Through seeking prayer, God will enlighten the eyes of your heart so that you will know the kingdom. Through seeking prayer, you will be drawn into deeper levels of obedience. "Not everyone who says to me, 'Lord, Lord,' will enter the kingdom of heaven, but only he who does the will of my Father who is in heaven" (Matthew 7:21).

Knock with a Persistent Faith

Knocking is an unspoken request for entrance to a place where entrance is otherwise denied. Where you have either the right or the ability to open a door, you don't have to knock. Knocking implies an intention, a certainty that you want entrance to a particular door. You want to gain access to the person behind the door. No one else will do. You have discovered the location of the person whom you seek, and now you will knock and keep on knocking until you have access.

To illustrate persevering faith, Jesus told this parable: "'Suppose one of you has a friend, and he goes to him at midnight and says, "Friend, lend me three loaves of bread, because a friend of mine on a journey has come to me, and I have nothing to set before him." Then the one inside answers, "Don't bother me. The door is already locked, and my children are with me in bed. I can't get up and give you anything." I tell you, though he will not get up and give him the bread because he is his friend, yet because of the man's boldness he will get up and give him as much as he needs'" (Luke 11:5–8).

The purpose of a parable is to illustrate one central truth. You cannot draw inferences about prayer from every detail of this story. The point is that this petitioner pinpointed the source of his supply and would not be dissuaded. The parable uses a central character who is opposite of God. This neighbor was surly and selfish. He was unwilling to give. Yet, even he was persuaded to give through persistence. The petitioner had enough faith in his neighbor to know that if he wouldn't give up, he would finally get what he needed. *How much more* will your Father, who longs to give, respond to your persistent faith.

All of the teaching about prayer is not contained in one parable or one passage. The teaching must be woven together and explained by the Holy Spirit. This one parable isolates and focuses on one aspect of prayer. It is meant to encourage you not to give up if you have to knock and keep on knocking. The answer is sure. Each prayer brings victory nearer. Each prayer is conquering unseen forces seeking to hinder the kingdom of God. Each prayer is mighty in its effect. God, unlike the dour neighbor, does not have to be persuaded. You can be more certain that He will meet your need than the parable's petitioner was that the neighbor could be worn down and persuaded.

Persevering Prayer Guided by the Spirit

You can only integrate these truths about persevering prayer into your life if you are praying in the Spirit. The unpretentious, determined, persistent faith of persevering prayer is based on knowing that God wants to give what you are asking. Persevering prayer will not change God or influence Him to do something outside

His perfect plan. Persevering prayer is not hardheaded, stubborn prayer. The very ability to persevere is implanted and nurtured by the Spirit.

Knowing the differences between Spirit-directed perseverance and self-directed stubborn praying is another lesson learned under the Spirit's tutelage. It is a matter of responding to your spiritual instincts rather than your intellectual understanding. "Trust in the Lord with all your heart and lean not on your own understanding; in all our ways acknowledge him, and he will make your paths straight" (Proverbs 3:5–6). This does not mean that your intellect has no place in prayer, but only when it has become the tool of the Spirit.

God Is Ready with the Answer

God knows what you need before you ask Him. (See Matthew 6:8.) Before you call, He has prepared the answer. You may be caught off guard in your need, but God is not. The purpose of your supplication is not to inform God. The purpose of your supplication is to accept that which God wants to offer.

One day one of my sons had an embarrassing incident occur at school. I was told about it by a neighbor who happened to see it. As soon as I heard, I knew that he needed to be encouraged and loved and would need me to help him put it into perspective. All day I planned how I could help him when he came home from school and told me about it. I was not only prepared, but eager, to help him.

To my surprise and disappointment, he did not tell me about it right away. I had determined that I should wait until he brought it up. It was several days before he told me. During those days I was longing to give him what he needed. I waited eagerly for him to give me access to his need. It was during these few days that God told me, "This is how I feel when you do not turn to Me in every need. I am overflowing with love toward you and long for you to come to Me and accept my provision for every detail of your life. I have everything prepared and am only waiting for you to ask."

The Book of James teaches that "you do not have, because you do not ask God" (James 4:2). The explanation James gives for asking and not receiving is because "you ask with wrong motives, that you may spend what you get on your pleasures" (James 4:3). This prayer problem is corrected when you are praying in the Spirit. This does not mean God never wants you to find pleasure in the answers He provides. The pleasure of which James is speaking is sensual pleasure. God's goals are more long-term than that. He wants you to find joy.

Sensual pleasure or momentary happiness is fleeting. It can be wiped away by circumstances or diminished by fluctuating emotions. God will form His plans to plant joy within you. Joy is delight rooted in the Holy Spirit. It exists through all circumstances. Joy is eternal. A deeper knowledge of God, a more complete obedience, a greater understanding of His ways will produce joy. God has a larger agenda when He provides for your needs and responds to your supplications. He will do so in such a way that your faith will be stretched and your joy in Him increased. He will hear your heart's cry and will respond to your genuine need. If your heart cries out for bread, He will not give you a stone. If your heart cries out for joy, He will not give you surface pleasure.

All of God's good gifts are contained in the Holy Spirit. "'If you then, though you are evil, know how to give good gifts to your children, how much more will your Father in heaven give the Holy Spirit to those who ask him!'" (Luke 11:13). It is the Spirit who is at work in your circumstances and on your behalf. It is the Holy Spirit who carries out the terms of God's covenant with you. He is God's answer to your every request.

Meditation

Father, thank You for my needs because they lead me to Your supply. Glorify Yourself through my needs. Most of all, Father, use my needs to establish Your kingdom and Your righteousness.

"And my God will meet all your needs according to his glorious riches in Christ Jesus" (Philippians 4:19).

Reflection

1. List your needs. Present each one to God for His supply.

2. Pray about each need with thanksgiving.

3. Stop and listen. What is God saying to you? Write it down.

Review

1. Does God want to meet your daily needs?

2. Is it appropriate to pray about your own needs?

3. Define asking prayer, seeking prayer, and knocking prayer.

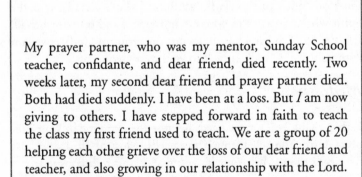

My prayer partner, who was my mentor, Sunday School teacher, confidante, and dear friend, died recently. Two weeks later, my second dear friend and prayer partner died. Both had died suddenly. I have been at a loss. But *I* am now giving to others. I have stepped forward in faith to teach the class my first friend used to teach. We are a group of 20 helping each other grieve over the loss of our dear friend and teacher, and also growing in our relationship with the Lord.
Annette Kristynik

Chapter 9

If Two Agree

"'Again, I tell you that if two of you on earth agree about anything you ask for, it will be done for you by my Father in heaven. For where two or three come together in my name, there am I with them" (Matthew 18:19–20).

In group intercession, you are the conductor of God's power. In a group of intercessors, the flow of God's power to earth is multiplied. The word Jesus used to define the agreement among intercessors means to harmonize or to blend. Our mutual prayers rise to God as a beautiful symphony. We do not become clones of one another. Our differences, disciplined and brought under the Spirit's control, add depth and richness to the prayer experience. As the instruments in an orchestra blend to produce one musical experience, so our finely tuned spirits blend to offer one prayer.

Small prayer groups are perfect settings to learn the secrets of harmonizing in prayer. Just like the Spirit of God teaches you as you pray alone, in your prayer closet (Matthew 6:6), He will teach you another dimension of praying as you join others. Becoming involved in a small prayer group involves commitment and risk. In a prayer group, you will learn to become open and honest about your needs. You will learn to build intimacy and trust in the name of Christ. You will have your vision expanded as you enter into the prayer burdens of others. In a prayer group, God will open your eyes to new ideas and needs through the experiences and insights of others.

Prayer Groups Born Out of Felt Need

My mother, Audrey, has had many prayer adventures through prayer groups over the past 25 years. It was about that long ago that she became involved in her first prayer group. Audrey was a lifelong Southern Baptist who always had a hunger for God and an active prayer life. With the sense that there was more to prayer than she knew, she joined three other women, each from different denominations, to begin praying as a group.

Before this small prayer group started, Audrey's experiences in group praying had not been encouraging. "In my experience, you went around the room and prayed in order. There were so many ways to be intimidated. If the person right before you said what you were going to say, then what? Or if someone prayed so eloquently and beautifully, how could you follow that? I was always busy listening to people's words, not to their prayers. I felt put on the spot. I felt it my Christian responsibility to come up with a good, heartfelt prayer."

When Audrey's first prayer group began, she didn't define it as a prayer group. They were a group of women who wanted to know more about prayer. They began to learn that they didn't have to use anyone's church or denominational language. They used conversational prayer. The women from this prayer group helped each other become aware of God in every situation. They helped each other tear down barriers to intimacy. When they were together, their attention was focused on realizing the power of God among them. Even when they were addressing each other in conversation, they knew that God was communicating through and among them. This group met weekly for years and still retain a deep bond today, even though the members live in different cities. They are still actively involved in prayer for one another.

Since then, Audrey has started three other prayer groups. Each one started when people felt a need to learn more about prayer and asked Audrey if she would help them. The second prayer group started when 3 women from three denominational backgrounds expressed to Audrey their hunger to know how to pray.

Eight women attended their first meeting. In a month attendance had grown to 32. They met weekly and soon expanded the time allotted from one hour to two. From this prayer group, a couples prayer group and another women's prayer group began. Audrey met weekly with the original group for 5 years, until she moved away. When she left, the groups were still going.

After living most of her adult life in one location, and having influenced many people and brought many into active and vital prayer groups, Audrey and my dad moved to another city. She spoke at a young women's meeting about her personal experiences in prayer and afterward several women asked her to disciple them in prayer. This was the beginning of another weekly prayer group. They met for several years and have been involved in many answers to prayers in their personal lives, in their church, on the missions field, and in the world. Fifteen years later, many of these women who were mentored by her in prayer, are committed intercessors and impact other lives in prayer.

Audrey, now in her 80s and faced with physical challenges that curb her activities, is still an active intercessor and encourager of others in prayer. She spends much time on the phone with people who need her prayers and her wisdom. One of the members of that early prayer threesome lives just down the hall from her and the other stays in close touch. Audrey, Tina, and Reba—all these years later have a deep bond that was forged in a small prayer group nearly 40 years ago. I want to be just like them when I grow up.

"In my experience," says Audrey, "prayer groups that work are formed on the basis of a need felt by several people to learn more about prayer. You can't form a prayer group because it's the right thing to do. I think the first step, if a person is feeling that need, is to ask God to lead her to others with the same desire. Ask God to bring the group together."

Getting Started

Based on Audrey's varied experiences in starting and leading prayer groups, she gives several practical suggestions. In her experience, it takes about three months for a group to solidify and begin to feel a oneness. There are several "prayer experiments" she suggests that might help that cohesiveness occur.

At the first meeting, have small purse-sized spiral notepads for every person. Pass them around and let each group member write her name, phone number, and address on a separate page in each person's pad. Each member then has a prayer page for every member. The first week's assignment is to pray daily for each group member. If you don't know a specific need, pray that God will bless her in a special way each day. The following week members can report on their experiences. This is the first step toward feeling connected to one another and involved in each others' lives.

For the second week, pass the notepads around again and write the names of family members. The second week's assignment is to pray for the family of each prayer group member during the week.

Next, help prayer group members begin to develop a spirit of praise and thanksgiving. The week's assignment might be to think of a person in your past who has influenced your spiritual life. Thank God for that person, then find the person and express your gratitude. This may involve a letter or a phone call. You will be calling attention to the grace of God expressed through others. In sharing those experiences, the group learns more about each other.

Another assignment might be to look for unexpected ways to express gratitude to someone. Look for the unappreciated people along your way and express your appreciation. This teaches you to be looking for reasons for thanksgiving and will have some exciting results. Have the group share their experiences at your next meeting.

Begin building trust by assigning prayer partners for a week. Have two people spend a few minutes getting to know each other and then have them pray together and thank God by name for the other person. Instruct them to pray for each other every day that week and suggest that they talk at least once. "Once you have committed someone to God, he or she will never look the same to you," says Audrey.

These "prayer experiments" help a new group develop group strength by being involved in a joint effort. They also teach prayer principles that will be incorporated into the prayer group experience. The assignments do not replace prayertime but are tools to help build a bond out of which a symphony of prayer will grow.

As time goes on, you probably won't need such structured activities. Intimacy and enthusiasm for prayer will take hold and things will flow naturally—or maybe *supernaturally* is the better word. Being involved in a small prayer group gives you the assurance that you are always being prayed for. When you are in need, there is a group of people who will voice your prayers to the Father. When you have a burden for a specific intercession, you have a group that will join their spirits with yours before the throne.

Prayer Groups Enrich the Prayer Experience

As the group matures, the praying becomes more honest and open. As the group's prayers are answered, there is a shared joy and excitement. "Answered prayer adds such joy to life," says Audrey. "When that answer is the result of our group's prayer, that joy is multiplied. Our bond is deepened. We can rejoice together." Audrey says that a few weeks before the Berlin Wall came down in 1989, a monumental event that even the most astute observers did not anticipate, one of their prayer group members was burdened about the situation, and they all joined her in intercession for the German people. On the day the wall came down, they felt a personal role in the history-making event. "We felt such joy in that event. We were seeing God's hand directing our prayers toward His ends. So many Christians are missing the joy of seeing answered prayer. Life is brightened and enhanced in every way by prayer."

When the praying moves beyond the bounds of personal needs and begins to encompass the world, a new interest in world events will develop. With today's technology, you can easily connect by email with missionaries or other people in locations you will not physically visit. You can form prayer partnerships with people in ministry around the world. You can impact the world through prayer. As Jesus teaches you to pray, reproducing His own heart in you, you will find that Jesus loves the world.

Prayer Groups Are Not Counseling Sessions

There are several things prayer groups need to guard against. One is the temptation to use your prayer group as an outlet for all your gripes. Prayer group is not a place to air your grievances, but a place to bring your burdens. When someone shares a burden, the group's responsibility is to take it to God. The temptation is to join in the misery, help her justify her attitude, give advice, or any number of natural responses. The only reason to enter into a discussion of a problem is to determine better how to pray. Only God has the answers.

Direct your prayers to God, not others. Don't use your prayers as a way to advise someone else. "Lord, help Mary to see that she needs to do so-and-so." Your job in prayer is not to tell God the solution, but to commit the problem.

Another trap to avoid is letting your prayer group become a fellowship group. The purpose of your time together should be prayer. From the moment you walk in, even while you are greeting each other and getting settled, you should be in a spirit of prayer. As God begins to move within your group, you will have no trouble. People will be eager to begin praying.

Personal burdens and needs are appropriate prayer requests at a small prayer group, but as the group matures, God will expand your prayer scope. For some, their involvement in a small group will be their introduction into intercession. Interceding for people with whom you have built trust and created a bond is a good starting place. As God answers prayers for your group, you will begin to reach out to the world. The world will become your personal concern. The Holy Spirit will begin to place His worldwide vision within your group.

Prayer Groups with Specific Focus

Some prayer groups are formed out of shared burdens of intercession for specific things. Missions prayer groups are made up of people who want to intercede with other Christians for needs on the missions field. Some people feel called to pray in groups for the needs of their own church. Other prayer groups are formed around a shared burden for spiritual awakening. Prayer for personal needs may take a backseat in this format.

Let's take a look at a few established prayer groups.

Ann's church was going through a hard time. It seemed the pastor was ill suited for the congregation. There was a great deal of backbiting and many broken relationships. The church was not growing in any way. Ann and her husband felt discouraged and seriously discussed changing churches. As she prayed about their decision, God led her to pray for her church and later to start a prayer group to undergird the church. The small prayer group met to pray for the church, but not criticize or ask God to change others. Each member of the group asked God to change her attitude and to bless their church in whatever way He wanted. They continued to meet regularly to pray for God's blessing on their church.

A year later, the pastor was called to a ministry position better suited to his gifts. God greatly blessed him in his new calling. The church called a new pastor who brought healing and growth to the church. The prayer group members continue to meet. They have a personal investment in the growth and ministry of their church.

Sue, Pat, Janet, and Lou formed a prayer group when they felt challenged to pray for their church. Their church had just appointed three strategic committees for enlarging and updating their facilities. The Deacon chairman asked the women to pray for those committees regularly and specifically as they were meeting. The chairperson of each committee calls the women to tell them when they will be meeting. As many as possible meet at the church and pray together during the committee meeting. "We feel that we are having a definite part in the planning as we meet and pray. We ask for harmony of spirit in our membership as we seek God's direction for our church and its future," says Sue.

These women also meet weekly for prayer on a wider scope. "We have seen God working in so many different situations. He answers in ways that we do not even think of asking, and that is a special joy. It is such a growing experience to share heartfelt thoughts in confidence and lift them up to the Lord. He truly has blessed each of us through this fellowship of prayer and praise, and it has been a walk in spiritual maturing."

Several women of Hill Baptist Church in Augusta, Georgia, met to pray regularly for missions. They had committed to intercede specifically for the ministry of missionary Becky Sumrall in New York. Becky ministers to people in lower income multi-family housing. Monica, the prayer group leader, called Becky before each prayer group meeting to get current prayer requests. She kept the requests in a prayer notebook so they could log their many specific answers to prayer. Once, Becky had spoken at their church and shown slides of her ministry. At the next meeting, one of the women in the prayer group felt led to pray for a little girl whose picture they had seen. The group joined her and they prayed for Shauna. The next time Monica called Becky to get updated prayer requests, Becky told her that one of the girls had accepted the Lord. "Which one?" asked Monica. "Her name is Shauna," Becky answered.

Another time, Becky asked the women to pray for a specific couple who seemed to have dropped out. When Monica called the next month, Becky was able to report, "They've been here every time the door is open." Time after time, Monica and the women who prayed with her had the privilege of seeing God's hand in Becky's ministry.

Once these women began their committed intercession, Becky saw funding and ministry opportunities open up. For example, there was a man in the complex for whom Becky had been praying. When his brother died, Becky saw an opportunity for ministry and went to his apartment. He was not home, but his girlfriend answered the door. The woman invited Becky in and told her, "I have been praying for three days that someone would come talk to me about God." Becky knew that the group's prayers were being answered daily in her ministry. The women prayed for her personal needs as well as her ministry needs. "Their commitment was supportive to me personally," says Becky. "Knowing they were interceding for me gave me the courage to continue to take risks in ministry."

In the fall of 1984, Fern Nichols's two oldest children of four were entering junior high school. Her heart was heavy and burdened with concern as she knew they would be facing their greatest test in resisting immoral values, vulgar language, peer pressure, and philosophies that would undermine their faith. She cried out to the Lord asking Him to protect them, enable them to see clearly the difference between right and wrong, and make good decisions.

The burden to intercede for her boys was overwhelming. She asked God to give her another mom who felt the same burden, and who would be willing to pray with her concerning their children and their school. God heard the cry of her heart and led her to another mom who shared her burden. Others were invited to come and they began meeting the following week for prayer.

This was the beginning of Moms in Touch International (MITI)—moms in touch with God, their children, their schools, and one another through prayer. As moms began sharing what God had been doing in their lives, and in the lives of their children through prayer, other groups began to spring up all over British Columbia where they were living at the time.

Summer 1985 brought a change to Fern's family as they moved from Abbotsford, British Columbia, to Poway, California. She soon discovered that God had given her still greater opportunities for carrying on the work that began in Canada. Once again she prayed that God would raise up moms who were willing to "stand in the gap" for their children. That fall, Fern began the first MITI group for Poway High School, and soon many other groups began to form for schools in that district. This grassroots effort spread quickly as moms prayed for groups to start around the state and across the nation.

Fall 1987 brought the first published Moms in Touch booklet, and in January 1988 the first Moms in Touch retreat was held with 35 women. They prayed for national exposure, and God answered their prayers that spring when Fern got a call from a producer at *Focus on the Family* and by May she and 12 other moms were on the air talking to Dr. Dobson! That first radio program brought over 20,000 responses.

Today, there are Moms in Touch groups in every state of the United States, and representatives in over 110 foreign countries around the world.

One group of four intercessors is very special to me. I am so grateful to have the women pray faithfully with me and for me about my ministry. They have been supporting me in this capacity for more than ten years. They are utterly faithful. I am always humbled by their willingness to meet and pray with me regularly. Their praying gives me courage. Everyone who comes into contact with this ministry through my writing or my speaking is the beneficiary of their faithful prayers. Joann Stokes, Wanda Kanai, Mary Medley, Mary Lee Butler—I just wanted you to know their names. If you are reading this book, then these women have prayed for you. They have prayed fervently and earnestly and regularly and with faith. You are touched by their lives, even if you never meet them.

One thing that always amazes me is how often insight comes through our praying. As we pray together, focused on letting the Holy Spirit awaken thoughts and direct our prayers, one or several of us will find ourselves praying a new thought, that turns out to be an answer we were looking for.

Joining with others to give specific focus to prayer for kingdom objectives is another step toward breaking out of small thinking that puts "me" as the center of the universe. As Jesus reproduces His own heart in you, recreating His intercession in you, you find that, while caring about even the hairs on your head, He also cares about the spread of His kingdom. What is in His heart begins to take root in your heart. Eventually you will find that the needs of others and the advance of God's kingdom are as important to you as your own personal needs.

The Family—a Ready-Made Prayer Group

My earliest lessons in prayer were during family devotions. I learned that every concern of mine was shared by my family and was a valid prayer request. I also learned that we were part of a larger network of Christians and, as such, shared burdens. I learned about intercession as I joined my parents in prayer for our church, our missionaries, individuals in need, and world affairs. Every evening my father read the names of the missionaries on the prayer calendar and we found the foreign countries on the family globe.

I don't want to leave the impression that these times were perfect. We squirmed, protested, and fought about whose turn it was to pray first. But we did it anyway. Those early experiences of family worship have given me a sense of my family as my prayer group. Although my parents, my two sisters, and I live in different cities, we are extremely close because we are a prayer group. We are open and honest with one another and keep in close touch because we are intercessors for each other.

I want the same thing for my sons. We used family devotions when they were young to introduce them to small-group praying.

They have a special bond with one another because of shared prayer burdens and answered prayers. They feel part of this ministry because they pray for it regularly.

As they have grown up, they have found a support network of praying friends wherever they go. The are instrumental in encouraging others to pray. Any leadership position they find themselves in, secular or religious, they instinctively know it is a platform from which to spread the kingdom.

How to Conduct a Prayer Group

When you meet as a group, you need to set a time limit for sharing prayer requests. Otherwise, you may spend the whole time taking prayer requests and not have time to pray. Prayer is the priority. Establish the first 20 minutes for any business, prayer requests, and answered prayers. One rule to help keep the prayer request time short is that no one comments on prayer requests. If you have had a similar experience or been in a similar situation, this is not the time to share. If you feel that your experience might be helpful, arrange another time to talk. You are not there to solve problems, but to commit them to God. This may seem structured, but you will find that it will keep your prayer session from turning into something else. Plan a time before or after prayer group for visiting. If you are a prayer group with a specific focus, the leader should have the prayer requests related to your focus prepared beforehand. Be aware—remind each other often—that even as you share prayer requests and updates, you are praying. God is already hearing it as prayer. He is right there among you and in you. He is part of your conversation.

Pray subject by subject. Introduce a subject and then let members pray sentence prayers as they feel led. A person can pray more than once, just like a person can enter a conversation more than once. Learn to pray conversationally. Keep prayers short and to the point. Eliminate religious-sounding phrases and long, flowery prayers.

Help group members feel comfortable with silence. One way to do this is to use visualization in praying. (This is not New-Age imaging or Eastern meditation. I will address this in the chapter on contemplative prayer.) As you introduce a subject for prayer, group members should visualize that person or situation in God's presence. This eliminates the need to fill up the silence and helps people focus their attention. People should only pray aloud if they want to. Help group members feel comfortable praying out loud or praying silently.

As you start, give your group time to solidify. Even people who have known each other for years may feel self-conscious in a prayer group together. Learning to pray as part of a group is a different experience from praying alone or leading public prayers. Many people will have to learn new attitudes toward praying out loud.

Keep in touch through the week. Assign prayer partners to commit to pray for each other every day. Work at building relationships outside the scheduled time. Be trustworthy. Never discuss personal prayer group matters outside the group.

You don't have to meet every week. My ministry prayer group meets once a month. With email and other technological advances, you can maintain close contact between times.

Although these are guidelines that many have found helpful, don't feel so structured that the Holy Spirit can't lead. Always be aware that the Holy Spirit will pray His desires through your group and will harmonize your spirits.

Meditation

Lord, we are gathered in Your name. Thank You for Your presence in our midst and Your power that is being poured into lives through our prayers. We are here to align our hearts with Yours. We are Your servants. Use us for Your glory. Harmonize our spirits so that we present to You a beautiful sound.

Reflection

1. Are your prayer group meetings truly times of prayer?

2. Has God begun to place His worldwide vision among you?

3. Stop and listen together. Share what God is saying to you.

Heart's Cry

Review

1. What is the purpose of a prayer group?

2. What are some traps for prayer groups to avoid?

3. Why are prayer groups important?

4. How can praying in a small group be important to your prayer life?

In my Girlfriends Prayer Group, we knew each other back in the days of babies, toddlers, not much money, and so on. It was really a friendship bonding time for all of us. We have now all moved to different cities and are spread out all over.

We hold a yearly get together where we spend time in prayer for our families and each month pray for one or two families. Requests are emailed and other needs may be received as they arise. It has been a blessing with many answered prayers and much waiting, but with a peace that God is in control. This past year we compiled a book of our experience in hopes that it would encourage others to follow.

Delores Burkett
Marietta, Georgia

Chapter 10

Upon This Rock

"On this rock I will build my church, and the gates of Hades will not overcome it. I will give you the keys of the kingdom of heaven; whatever you bind on earth will be bound in heaven, and whatever you loose on earth will be loosed in heaven" (Matthew 16:18–19).

The church is God's expression of Himself in the world. The church is the physical presence of Christ on earth. The church is the full expression of Christ. God does not intend that an individual believer's prayer life will reach its full potential outside the context of the church. When we do battle with the spiritual forces of evil in the heavenly realms, it is to be as a church. The church has the authority to speak the will of God into the spiritual world. "For our struggle is not against flesh and blood, but against the rulers, against the authorities, against the powers of this dark world and against the spiritual forces of evil in the heavenly realms. . . . His intent was that now, through the church, the manifold wisdom of God should be made known to the rulers and authorities in the heavenly realms, according to his eternal purpose which he accomplished in Christ Jesus our Lord" (Ephesians 6:12; 3:10–11). The prayers of the church set in motion the spiritual forces to accomplish God's will and establish His kingdom. The keys to unlock and unleash the kingdom of heaven belong to the church.

Individuals Fused into One Body

The Holy Spirit indwells every believer. God works through His Spirit in the individual lives of believers. The personal, private prayer life of each individual is imperative. Each believer is individually accountable to God for his or her life. However, no believer will reach full maturity in Christ apart from the church. It is Christ Himself who gives gifts to the church, embodied in men and women, "to prepare God's people for works of service, so that the body of Christ may be built up until we all reach unity in the faith and in the knowledge of the Son of God and become mature, attaining to the whole measure of the fullness of Christ" (Ephesians 4:12–13). We are one in Him who indwells our separate lives. Each individual's spiritual life flows into the life of the church. Jesus's prayer for His followers is that we will be one just as the Father and Son are one. (See John 17:11, 21–23.) This is the content of His eternal intercession. We are to function as one being, infused with one life, intent on one purpose. This fusion of separate parts into one integrated whole is a divine act. Humans can come together to form an organization, but only the Spirit of God can give birth to a church. The role of the church is to establish the will of God in the spiritual realm through prayer, and establish the kingdom of God on earth through ministry and witness.

The picture of the church that Scripture paints is the picture of a body with Jesus as its head. I saw a parable of the church during my husband's illness. Because he had brain cancer, the illness he had was only in his brain. The type of cancer he had never moves from the brain to any other part of the body. Yet, the illness shut down his whole body. I wrote the following in my journal:

> Wayne, because he is not able to exercise discipline over his brain right now, does not know he has a left side again. It is foreign to him. In the course of his hallucinating, he looks at his left hand and says, "What is that?" Once he called me from across the room and said, "Jennifer! You need to move your hand. It's in my way!" Several times I have seen him lift his left hand with his right hand and try to move it out of his way as if it were an object sitting on his lap. How

strange that his hand is connected to his body in every way except that it is not receiving signals from his brain.

As I watched Wayne today, grieved as I was, I could not help but think about the way the Scripture describes the relationship between Christ and His followers. He is the Head and we are the body. See how totally each part of the body is dependent upon the Head? He moves through His believers and His desires and will are exercised through His followers. Without the Head, the hand cannot be the hand; the foot cannot be the foot. The apostle Paul wrote about a follower who starts living as if he or she were in charge. "He has lost connection with the Head, from whom the whole body, supported and held together by its ligaments and sinews, grows as God causes it to grow" (Colossians 2:19). A body part disconnected from its Head is lifeless—as useless as if it belonged to someone else.

The Church Must Be Purified

In the same way that individuals must be refined and purified by the Refiner's Fire in order to be conductors of the will of God, so must the church. Everything that is true in the lives of individual intercessors is true in the life of the church. Jesus gave His life for the church "to make her holy, cleansing her by the washing with water through the word, and to present her to himself as a radiant church, without stain or wrinkle or any other blemish, but holy and blameless" (Ephesians 5:26–27). His goal is that His church should radiate His life.

The first step in becoming a praying church is to ask the Father to fill you, as a church, with His Spirit. Ask Him to come into your midst as the Refiner's Fire. Relationships must be restored, pride put to death, priorities reordered, lives adjusted. The Holy Spirit must be given access to every area of your church's life. You must be willing to be swept clean so that the life of Christ can be expressed through you.

The institutional church is made up of human beings with varying degrees of commitment to Christ, with a wide range of backgrounds and personality types and interests. By design, the eternal church consists of a variety of gifts and passions, each imparted by the Holy Spirit. Only by supernatural work of God can this disparate group of people—many at odds with each other—become a whole, functioning body. Since God commands us to be as one, and Jesus is praying that we may be as one, then we *can* be as one.

The Church Accesses Eternal Resources

All of the resources of heaven are dispensed through the Son. "For God was pleased to have all his fullness dwell in him" (Colossians 1:19). "For no matter how many promises God has made, they are "Yes" in Christ" (2 Corinthians 1:20). The fullness of God dwells in the Son; the fullness of the Son dwells in the church. "And God placed all things under his feet and appointed him to be head over everything for the church, which is his body, the fullness of him who fills everything in every way" (Ephesians 1:22–23).

According to Ephesians 1, Christ is above all rule and authority and power and dominion. All things are in subjection to Christ. Christ, supreme ruler of the universe and reservoir of the riches of God, is head of the church. The church is His body. He expresses His life through the church. The riches of God flow through Christ; the riches of Christ flow through the church. What a tragedy it is that many churches are spending more time in committee meetings and budget disputes and building programs than in prayer. If the church would take seriously her mandate to let the riches of heaven flow through her to the world, the possibilities are limitless. If we, the church, would come together in prayer and obedience, would take up arms against the enemy, would intercede for the souls of people and the fate of nations, the gates of hell could not prevail against us.

When Frank Lewis arrived in Nevada to pastor Green Valley Baptist Mission, land for a building looked like an impossibility. Green Valley is an affluent community development outside Las Vegas. The developer specifically did not want a Southern Baptist church there. The areas zoned for churches were four acres, maximum. The cost of four acres of raw, undeveloped land would be $160,000 to $260,000, depending on location. Frank went to meet the developer and established a relationship. The developer asked Frank how his church would benefit the community. Frank shared his plans and told the developer that Green Valley Baptist Mission was there to be a friend to the community. After that, the board of directors decided to sell the mission four acres of land for $160,000 and donate half of that to the mission as a charitable contribution. Green Valley had been on the state prayer calendar that year. Churches all over Nevada were praying for the need listed as their primary concern—to purchase land for a building.

I first wrote this book in the summer of 1991. We were living in times of breathtaking change in the world order. Every week held new surprises. The Iron Curtain, once thought to be impenetrable, had been torn apart. The world was open to the gospel. Historians, news commentators, specialists in world affairs, all were taken by surprise. They had no idea that for decades the church had been interceding for just such impossibilities. That which could not have been accomplished through men had been accomplished through the prayers of the church. I had no idea how events would unfold. But right then the gospel was reaching into corners of the earth that were closed before. The Holy Spirit had been at work, through the prayers of the church, preparing hearts for the gospel and strengthening His people who had been oppressed by their governments. For me, the nightly news was testimony to the power of God through the prayers of His church.

In 1991, Willow Creek Baptist Church in Fort Worth, Texas, was a young church, but already its effect was being felt around the world. The members of Willow Creek accepted an assignment to intercede for an unreached group of people in a remote part of China. Members prayed individually and on the first Sunday of every month they interceded corporately. Recently, one of their church members met some Christians from Russia who had heard that an evangelistic film was being translated into the language of the group of people for whom they had been praying. This group would hear the gospel for the first time.

First Baptist Church of Pinevelle, Louisiana, agreed to pray for an unreached group of people in the former USSR. Baptist Women prayer groups took it as a special assignment. Sunday School classes, especially the class of internationals, interceded. The entire church prayed for a group of people they had never heard of before. At that time, it seemed nearly impossible that the gospel would penetrate this group of people. Soon after that, the deputy minister of education of this group came to Pineville, Louisiana, with an interpreter to explore the possibility of an exchange program. While there, the group met with a retired professor, a native of the then USSR and a Christian, who gave them Bibles in their own language. They took the Bibles home with them. The representatives were not Christians, as far as anyone knew. We can only speculate about what God may be doing. Through the prayers of the church, two people from a faraway country came to a small town in Louisiana and took home Bibles in their own language.

I am revising and updating this book in fall of 2006. The world events that so amazed us all those years ago, now we take for granted. The areas that are closed to the gospel today are areas most of us barely knew about 15 years ago. Yet, world events conspire to open avenues for the gospel to be taken to every corner of the world. Right now, the United States is formally at war in Afghanistan and Iraq. The carnage is heartbreaking. The emotional and economic stress on the global community is escalating. War is dreadful. Yet, somewhere buried under all the headlines and news video, somewhere in the rubbish heap of heartache, God is at work advancing His kingdom. Heart by heart, life by life.

Was there ever a time when the church needed to be praying more than in these days? Political leaders are making decisions never before contemplated in our history. We must be praying for their wisdom. Laws are being passed and other laws considered that will fundamentally alter our society. For better or for worse, only God knows. No one is wise enough to see the future ramifications. We can only speculate. It is imperative, it is crucial, it is essential—and any other word you can come up with—that the church be praying. Not praying our opinions, but praying the power and wisdom and provision and protection of God.

Frank Laubauch in *Prayer: The Mightiest Force in the World* says, "Most of us will never enter the White House and offer advice to the President. Probably he will never have time to read our letters. But we can give him what is far more important than advice. We can give him a lift into the presence of God, make him hungry for divine wisdom, which is the grandest thing one man ever does of another. We can visit the White House with prayer *as many times a day as we think of it,* and every such visit makes us a channel between God and the President."

God Reveals Himself to the Praying Church

Henry Blackaby wrote a book called *What the Spirit Is Saying to the Churches.* In it he tells the story of Faith Baptist Church in Saskatoon, Saskatchewan, Canada. This is a church who committed themselves to seeking and following God. Their obedience is a challenge to every church. Through the Spirit-directed ministries of this tiny congregation, thousands have come to Christ. Here is a part of their story:

"One of the most amazing discoveries in our walk with God as a church was how open-ended, and full, and never-ending were the consequences of following Him. We learned that what issued from God continues eternally when we become part of His activity.

"For instance, an obedient ministry to students led to the salvation of many students. Among them were Gerry and Connie Tafflon. Each was saved and baptized in our church when single. God later led them to be married. Gerry soon felt called of God into the ministry. Our convention called him to serve as our first catalytic missionary to Montreal, Quebec. Because of Gerry's French-Canadian background, he is now our first missionary to French-speaking Canadians, and will be a catalyst for the beginning of many French Canadian Baptist churches, and the calling out of many who shall go across our world to other French-speaking countries as well. What began as a faithful response to God's invitation to witness on a campus has resulted in a timeless, continuous activity of God. We could never have imagined how far-reaching would be God's activity when Gerry and Connie came to know Christ as Lord."

God is seeking churches who will follow Him, who will seek His face, and who will carry out His ministry in the world.

Meditation

Lord, we are Your body on this earth. Your physical body was not sleek and pampered, but broken and spilled out for us. Forgive us for assuming that we are to be comfortable and rich and spoiled.

Forgive us for not wanting to be bothered with that which concerns You. Forgive us for trying to put You on display instead of taking You into the world. Forgive us for using You as a marketing tool, and not being willing to be broken and spilled out too.

"And he took bread, gave thanks and broke it, and gave it to them saying, 'This is my body given for you'" (Luke 22:19).

Reflection

1. As a member of the body of Christ, are you merging your life with fellow Christians?

2. Stop and listen. What is God saying to you? Write it down.

Review

1. What is the church?

2. What is the church's role in prayer?

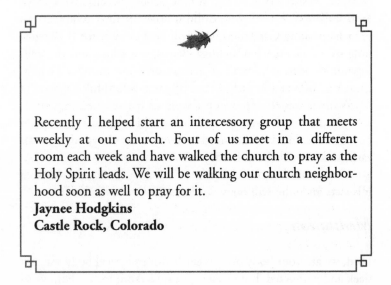

Recently I helped start an intercessory group that meets weekly at our church. Four of us meet in a different room each week and have walked the church to pray as the Holy Spirit leads. We will be walking our church neighborhood soon as well to pray for it.
Jaynee Hodgkins
Castle Rock, Colorado

Chapter 11

Be Still and Know

"Be still, and know that I am God; I will be exalted among the nations, I will be exalted in the earth" (Psalm 46:10).

We live in a world full of noise. Technology has made it possible for us to banish silence from our lives completely. We can get lost in the noises around us and never have to listen to the silence. We live in a world of activities. We admire those who never have a spare minute. Busy means important. We rush through our days stalked by burnout and stress. We don't know what to do with stillness.

God calls us to silence, inner as well as outer. He invites us to listening prayer. He calls us to be refreshed by His presence. He calls us to take time to experience Him in the inner sanctuary of our souls. He draws us to rest from the strife around us in the shelter of His presence. "You hide them in the secret place of Your presence from the conspiracies of man; You keep them secretly in a shelter from the strife of tongues" (Psalm 31:20 NASB).

Listening prayer is the ground from which spoken prayer grows. Spoken prayer will not reach its fullness unless it is born in listening prayer.

The Secret Place of the Most High

"[He] who dwells in the secret place of the Most High shall abide under the shadow of the Almighty" (Psalm 91:1 NKJV). Secrets are for trusted friends. Telling someone a secret implies confidence and intimacy. Most people who know me know only the things I tell openly about myself. Only my closest companions know my secrets. God wants you to know His secrets. "The Lord confides in those who fear him; he makes his covenant known to them" (Psalm 25:14). "He takes the upright into his confidence" (Proverbs 3:32).

Secrets are usually whispered. You have to listen closely to hear a secret. Secrets are not exchanged in the hustle-bustle of life. Secrets are exchanged in quiet places, during quiet moments. God wants you to meet Him in His secret place to listen for His whisper.

God's secret place is His presence (Psalm 31:20). The way into His presence is through Jesus. The place of His presence is within you. You will find Him at the center of your being. He has erected His tabernacle in your soul. The veil has been torn away and His presence is beckoning you and drawing you. He has secrets to tell.

Listening Prayer

God has things to tell you. He wants you to listen. He wants to tell you great and mighty things that you have not known (Jeremiah 33:3). Isn't that what a secret is? Something you didn't know before? Look at God's invitation.

"Call to me and I will answer you and tell you great and unsearchable things you do not know" (Jeremiah 33:3). I'm going to restate this sentence pulling in the layers of meaning in the Hebrew words from which this was translated. "Have an encounter with Me and call Me by name. I will respond by speaking out and announcing to you—clarifying for you and explaining to you—matters that are beyond your knowledge and too advanced for you to find out for yourself. I will tell you things you did not know and cannot know unless I reveal them to you."

When we learn the art of silence, then we create the setting in which God can reveal to us His secrets. He wants you to be so close to Him that He can tell you about things that are in His heart.

He wants you to be still before Him, to come to Him in receptive silence. He wants you to hear on the deepest level. "'Listen and understand'" (Matthew 15:10).

We are not programmed for silence. It does not come naturally to sit quietly in God's presence without words. Listening to God is a learned discipline.

I find it helpful to visualize the presence of God. This is something totally different from imaging, transcendental meditation, or visualization techniques used in New Age or Eastern religions. In visualizing God's presence, you are not helping God answer your prayers. You are not creating cosmic energy. You are simply using pictures instead of words. God used visual images to help His people understand Him: the tabernacle, a burning bush, a pillar of fire by night, and a cloud by day. The presence of God is a reality, not something you wish to create. Mentally picturing the presence of God is one way to focus your mind on Him without words.

You may picture His presence on His throne as described in Revelation. You may picture Him as fire or light. He does not want us to limit Him to a physical form and worship that form, but He has given pictures of Himself to describe different aspects of His being. No mental image could ever capture the full essence of God. The point is not to create an image to worship, but to find a way to center your thoughts on God. As you visualize the presence of God, visualize yourself in that presence. You should, mentally or physically, kneel before Him. Since Jesus is the way into His presence, I often visualize Jesus leading me there and then taking His place at the right hand of the Father.

In His presence, I feel the need to empty myself. I visualize placing things on His altar: my pride, my specific desires, my family, my specific worries or burdens, my ministry. I let the Holy Spirit put His finger on areas that need to be placed on the altar. Then, when I feel emptied of myself, I spend time praising Him. Praise is especially meaningful in this face-to-face time. Then I am quiet and only speak in response to Him.

What comes from these times of worship and adoration and listening varies. Listening prayer gives God access to me. I don't hear God's voice thundering out information. He doesn't tell me what day the world is going to end or become my fortune-teller. Often, a Scripture comes to mind with fresh meaning as it relates to me. I respond to Him based on what He has said through that Scripture. Sometimes a sin or weakness comes to mind, and I repent and experience His cleansing. Sometimes I am filled with the sense of His love and hear Him speak it directly to me. Other times I hear Him encouraging me. At times, He gives me a specific command to obey. His communication is quiet and intimate and is spoken into my understanding.

Listening Prayer Kindles Love

It is in the context of listening prayer that a deep sense of your love for God is kindled. Love is a natural response to the presence of God. He is love and your love for Him comes from His love for you. "This is love: not that we loved God, but that he loved us. . . . We love because he first loved us" (1 John 4:10, 19).

If you don't feel the emotion of love toward God, it might be because you have not consistently spent time focused on His presence. You don't need to measure your emotions and gauge your love by how you feel. Love is really expressed in obedience. But God wants you to have that joy of feeling great love for Him. He wants to reproduce His heart of love in you. He is the starting point of all love. In His presence, He imparts love.

Love for God translates into love for people. "Dear friends, since God so loved us, we also ought to love one another. No one has ever seen God; but if we love one another, God lives in us and his love is made complete in us" (1 John 4:11–12).

Whom does God love?

He loves sinners.
"But God demonstrates his own love for us in this: While we were still sinners, Christ died for us" (Romans 5:8).

"Christ Jesus came into the world to save sinners—of whom I am the worst. But for that very reason I was shown mercy so that in me, the worst of sinners, Christ Jesus might display his unlimited patience as an example for those who would believe on him and receive eternal life" (1 Timothy 1:15–17).

He loves His children.
"How great is the love the Father has lavished on us, that we should be called children of God! . . . This is how we know what love is: Jesus Christ laid down his life for us" (1 John 3:1, 16).

"Greater love has no one than this, that he lay down his life for his friends" (John 15:13).

He loves the people of all the nations.
"May the nations be glad and sing for joy, for you rule the peoples justly and guide the nations of the earth" (Psalm 67:4).

He loves the people who walk in darkness.
"The people walking in darkness have seen a great light; on those living in the land of the shadow of death a light has dawned" (Isaiah 9:2).

He loves His enemies.
"Love your enemies and pray for those who persecute you, that you may be sons of your Father in heaven" (Matthew 5:44–45).

"Jesus said, 'Father, forgive them, for they do not know what they are doing'" (Luke 23:34).

If He is reproducing His love in your heart, then whom will you come to love? This is not a exhaustive list, of course. But you can see that the Holy Spirit, pouring the Father's love into your heart, will be calling you to pray for the very people the Father loves. "God has poured out his love into our hearts by the Holy Spirit, whom he has given us" (Romans 5:5).

In your listening prayer, God may ask you to bring someone to His throne. Bathed in His light, you will see that person from a new perspective. God will fill you with supernatural love that defies understanding. God's love for that person will flow through you. Listen to what God wants to say about that person. He will open your eyes to hidden potential. He will help you replace judgment with mercy. He will show you the tiny, hidden spark of Himself in that person.

Charles Swindoll in *Simple Faith* says, "True love possesses the ability to see beyond. In that sense we might say that love has x-ray vision. It goes beyond mere words. It sees beneath the veneer. Love focuses on the soul. Love sees another's soul in great need of help and sets compassion to work. I think of the late Corrie ten Boom and her response to the Nazi guards who had brutalized her sister. She was able to forgive them. She refused to live the rest of her life brimming with resentment and bitterness. True love sees beyond the treatment that it endures. True love doesn't need agreement to proceed. True love goes on against all odds. That is why Jesus simply says, Love them."

Prayer in response to the Father's call to love is one of the surest ways to find relationships restored. It is one of the most straightforward paths to being freed of resentment and anger and hurt. An amazing thing, the by-product of responsive prayer.

Listening Prayer Releases Creativity

God is Creator. He is the only true creative being. Only He made something from nothing. All other creativity stems from His creation. The source of all creativity invites you to listen to Him.

Your creativity is stymied by preconceived ideas, distorted information, insecurity, stress, and any number of other things. God wants to release His own creativity in you. He wants to remove all barriers to creativity and free you to think and dream outside the false parameters constructed in your thinking. He wants to give you fresh ideas and insights, new ways to minister, new ways to reflect Him in your daily life. He wants to tell you His secrets.

In waiting before Him, adoring Him, worshipping Him, your spirit is renewed. He will satisfy your thirsty spirit and fill you with Himself, the Creator. "'If anyone is thirsty, let him come to me and drink. Whoever believes in me, as the Scripture has said, streams of living water will flow from within him.' By this he meant the Spirit" (John 7:37–39). The Holy Spirit will gush out of your life in wellsprings of creative love. In His presence, your potential in the Holy Spirit is unleashed.

I love long, solitary drives. It's an oddball thing about me. When I feel that I can spare the time, I drive to speaking events and to see friends and family across the country. I could get there faster if I flew, but the long drive is restful and quiet and excellent listening time. I like the total silence. On those drives is where most of my new ideas come from. I get new thoughts and insights about Scripture I have been studying. I have new ideas, one tripping over another, about the ministry. I write poetry and come up with new book ideas. If I've been on a long driving trip, my staff knows to be ready when I come home to start on new things. I love the creativity that comes out of listening.

Listening Prayer Dissolves Fear

"Perfect love drives out fear" (1 John 4:18). God is perfect love. Fear cannot exist in His presence. His presence drives out fear. Fear exists when God is not seen clearly. Fear takes hold when the truth about God has been obscured or distorted. When you listen to Him, you will hear Him say directly to you, "'Do not fear, for I am with you; do not be dismayed, for I am your God. I will strengthen you and help you; I will uphold you with my righteous right hand'" (Isaiah 41:10).

If you read this verse from Isaiah in the context of the history of Israel, it would inform you of God's might and His constant love for His people. It would inform you of His power to save and deliver. It would inform you of His personal attention to the needs of His called-out ones. If, in contrast, you listen as God speaks these words to you, fear loses its hold and is exiled from your situation by the powerful presence of the Most High.

Listening Prayer Establishes Peace

"You will keep in perfect peace him whose mind is steadfast, because he trusts in you. Trust in the Lord forever, for the Lord, is the Rock eternal" (Isaiah 26:3–4). Turmoil and the Rock eternal cannot coexist. The person whose mind is steadfastly fixed on God is kept in perfect peace. Listen as He speaks peace. "I will listen to what God the Lord will say; he promises peace to his people, his saints" (Psalm 85:8).

God speaks peace. You cannot establish peace in your spirit by learning about peace or by looking on the bright side or by pretending peace. God establishes peace and He does so by speaking. His word of peace finds its home in the spirit of the listener.

Sometimes I have swirling anxiety. As pressure mounts from different directions, I just let it congregate. I find myself generally agitated, without knowing a specific cause. At those times, I stop and get my journal and listen to the Lord. I write down a list of everything that I'm anxious or tense about. That helps me clarify and name my problem. I trust the Holy Spirit to help me realize the issues. Then I go back through my list and by each thing I write, "Yours." It is a commitment ceremony for me. I hear the voice of my Father saying, "Don't worry. I've thought of everything!" Or maybe He'll say, "I'm more powerful than any of these things, and I'm watching your back." He just says what I need to hear, and His voice speaks peace into my heart. I just can't remain anxious when I am fully present with Him.

Does a storm rage in your spirit? Is your mind in turmoil? Are your emotions being driven and tossed by the wind? Stop and listen. He is speaking peace.

Listening Amid the Noise

Listening prayer may occur during extended or compact time periods. The experiences of others who have been used mightily in intercession teach that you should schedule extended periods of listening prayer on a regular basis. This requires finding a time and a place to pray without interruption. However, you can be listening to God at all times in your spirit. You can live in a state of receptivity to His voice. You can mentally bring yourself into His presence often throughout the day. You can inwardly return to Him every time you realize you have stepped away from the Holy Spirit. Everything your physical ears hear can be filtered through your spiritual ears. Listening to God is not an elaborate ceremony, but a way of living. We are always in a listening frame of mind and God is speaking to us in ways that we will recognize if we will be alert.

Would you indulge me one more time and let me share from my journal what the Lord showed us about our intimacy with Him during my husband's illness?

Last night Wayne began to be responsive again. I sat by him in the bed and held his hand and the boys sat around his bed. We talked and Wayne would squeeze his response, and I would pass it on. We really had a pretty good idea about what he was responding, even though it was a sparse form of communication. The reason is that we had hours and hours and years and years of previous conversations, and we have history and intimacy. So a hand-squeeze can speak volumes. We knew exactly how his voice would sound if he spoke what his squeeze was meant to say. We could hear him without hearing him.

Someone else might have held Wayne's hand and felt his squeeze, but would not be able to "hear his voice" in that squeeze because the relationship is missing. The intimacy is missing. How valuable, in retrospect, are the many conversations over the years—some long and intense, but most were conversations as we lived our lives, on the go, in the context of the moment. Now all woven together into a masterpiece of love.

I thought this morning about how God is always talking to us, always communicating in little ways. If we have history and intimacy with Him, if we have spent time carefully listening to Him, then we will be hearing from Him continually. Because of our intimacy with Him, we will experience the squeeze of His hand as our hand rests in His. We will feel His little nudges and see the twinkle in His eye. Volumes of communication can be expressed in a nanosecond. We can hear His voice.

Intercession Without Words

At times, mentally picturing the presence of God in a situation or with a person can express your intercession. For example, when I would think of my children at school during the day, I pictured Jesus beside them, whispering to them or holding their hands. This is a picture Jesus painted for me by saying, "I am with [them] always." This is the truth. My mental image of it does not make it the truth, but helps me experience the truth. I am not hampered in my intercession by not being able to think of the right words, or because I don't know someone's minute-by-minute needs. As I hold this truth in a mental picture, the Holy Spirit is articulating my heart's cry.

When I pray for the President or other national and world leaders, I picture Jesus there with them. When I pray for missionaries, I think of Jesus ministering there through them. When I pray for my pastor as he preaches, I visualize Jesus standing with him or walking among the congregation touching those in need. If I am praying for someone who is sick, I visualize Jesus placing His hands on that person.

(**Author's note:** Here is a personal opinion on using visualization in prayer. I have heard it suggested that you visualize your prayer answered the way you want it to be. For example, if you are praying for someone to be healed, visualize that person well. I disagree with that concept. It seems to imply that your visualization imparts power or will bring your desires into being. I'm sure that is not the intent, but I personally feel uncomfortable with it.)

This kind of praying can be wordless or can be incorporated into spoken prayer. This kind of prayer, initiated and controlled by the Holy Spirit, can eliminate the problem some people have in extended praying or in waiting on God.

The Inner Circle

Jesus has pulled you into His inner circle, those to whom He will impart His secrets. Listen. "'I have called you friends, for everything that I learned from my Father I have made known to you'" (John 15:15). A person who is following a doctrine need not listen. There is nothing new to know. The one who is following Christ must be continually listening. Spoken prayer is your response to what you have heard. Any other kind of speaking on your part can only be an attempt to instruct God.

This should not be restrictive for your prayer life. It should be freeing. It frees you from the responsibility of deciding what God should do. Many times when people say, "I can't pray because I don't know what to pray," they mean, "I haven't decided how to instruct God in this matter."

As you adopt a listening posture as your way of living your life, you will find that God is always speaking to you. The prayer that comes to your lips, it turns out, is the prayer that God has awakened in you. You don't have to hear Him say sentences to hear Him. He whispers, and it echoes in your heart.

God—the Listening Father

There are times, however, when words of pain or anger or disillusionment pour out of you. God invites this. "Take words with you and return to the Lord" (Hosea 14:2). You don't have to edit yourself or repress your true feelings in His presence. He wants you to pour your feelings out in words to Him so that He can heal and restore. Read the Psalms. There is no formula for prayer. The same one who prayed, "Praise the Lord, O my soul; all my inmost being, praise his holy name. Praise the Lord, O my soul, and forget not all his benefits" (Psalm 103:1–2), also prayed, "Listen to my prayer, O God, do not ignore my plea; hear me and answer me. My thoughts trouble me and I am distraught" (Psalm 55:1–2).

God is always listening for your cry. "Arise, cry out in the night, as the watches of the night begin; pour out your heart like water in the presence of the Lord" (Lamentations 2:19). The key is, don't pour out words and walk away. As you pour out words, He pours in healing. He hears beyond your words. Pour out your heart in His presence, and then listen. Continue to pour out your heart, for days or weeks or months, until your heart begins to pour out hope. Then you will know that healing has begun.

"Find rest, O my soul, in God alone; my hope comes from him. He alone is my rock and my salvation; he is my fortress, I will not be shaken. My salvation and my honor depend on God; he is my mighty rock, my refuge. Trust in him at all times, O people; pour out your hearts to him, for God is our refuge" (Psalm 62:5–8).

Meditation

Father, push back the noise. Your secrets come wrapped in silence.

Reflection

Schedule one full hour to spend in listening prayer. Visualize the presence of God. Let the Holy Spirit guide you. Find a guide for how to spend an hour in prayer at www.hearts-cry.net. You can download it at no cost.

Review

1. What is listening prayer?

2. What role can listening prayer play in your life?

We have a Front Line Prayer Team that meets every Sunday morning from 7:30 *a.m.* until our service begins. This has proven to be powerful for the entire Sunday worship service. Attitudes are being changed. Minds are being transformed. The Holy Spirit is convicting. The Spirit of God is in our building. You can feel God's presence!

I am involved with a weekly Bible study, and we prayed for the specific people that God wanted in this study. We prayed for the location. We pray in that home, around it, and over that family continually.

Tamara Blatny
Blue Springs, Missouri

Chapter 12

Draw Aside

"After he had dismissed them, he went up on a mountainside by himself to pray. When evening came, he was there alone" (Matthew 14:23).

J esus's habit during His earthly life was to draw aside to pray. He prayed with His disciples, He prayed in the synagogue, He prayed spontaneously in front of followers, He led public prayers, but habitually He prayed alone.

Although prayer cannot be squeezed into a space of time, there must be disciplined daily prayertimes. Your praying should be continual. Yet it must be nurtured in scheduled times set aside for prayer. Early morning seems to be the best time. Jesus got up long before daybreak and went into the mountains to pray. In reading about the lives of people of prayer, it seems that they always prayed in the early morning hours before anyone else was awake. Certainly you can schedule your prayertime any time of the day. However, many people find this to be a time of the day when they are not interrupted. It is difficult to begin getting up early enough to pray, but not impossible. If you continue in the practice for a period of time, your body clock will readjust itself, and you will find yourself going to bed earlier and getting up more easily. It is a choice you make.

Setting Aside the Time

Make a firm decision that you will set aside a time for daily prayer. Decide on the hour. Write it on your schedule. You have agreed to meet God alone at that hour so consider it a firm commitment. Give Him the same respect and consideration you would anyone with whom you have an appointment. When you are struggling with the decision to get out of bed for your appointment with God, stop and listen. Hear Him say, "Come and meet Me. I have wonderful things to tell you. I am looking forward to our time together." Remember that you are responding to His voice rather than fulfilling a duty.

Designate a place. Don't be so tied to that location that you miss your prayertime when that place is unavailable. It is good to have the logistics worked out so that there are fewer decisions to distract you from your purpose. If you keep your Bible, your journal or prayer list, a writing tool, and your missionary prayer calendar in your place, you won't have to waste time gathering your materials.

Have a plan in mind. This will keep you from getting to your prayer place and thinking, "Well, here I am. What now?" A clear plan will get you started and keep you focused. It is not to replace the Holy Spirit's leadership.

Organizing Your Intercession

Break your intercession list into days. Some people you will pray for daily. Others you will pray for weekly. This assures that you can give ample time in intercession for each subject. You would be overwhelmed if you tried to intercede for every need every day. Again, this is just an outline. This should not replace your commitment to rely on God to direct your praying.

Have a page in your prayer notebook for each topic of intercession. Record needs, answers, insights, Scriptures, or prayers. Use a loose-leaf notebook so that you can add pages. Keep a section of your notebook to record what God is saying to you about your life. This will become a record of your experience with God.

How to Spend an Hour in Prayer

Here is a suggestion for how you might structure a prayertime. Perhaps by using this outline, you will feel less overwhelmed and more motivated to begin.

1. Begin with listening prayer. Visualize yourself in God's presence. Worship Him with your praise and thanksgiving. Wait in silence until you feel ready to move on. This may be a minute or two or may take your whole prayer hour. Ask God to show you anything that is hindering the flow of Christ's life through you. At any time during your prayer hour that a sin is brought to your mind, stop then and deal with it. Keep the channel clear.

2. Next, spend time reading the Bible. It is best to have a plan for Bible reading. You will not have to be distracted from your focus by deciding where to read. As you begin, expect God to speak to you. Sometimes He will speak more distinctly than other times. Don't set up expectations for exactly how He will speak—like He spoke to someone else or like He spoke to you another time. Let God communicate in His own way.

3. After you have listened to God through His Word, begin your intercession. Still visualizing yourself in God's presence, take each burden to Him. Trust Him to pour His thoughts through you. Let your mind be the Holy Spirit's instrument. As you pray in each situation, you are the conductor of God's will and God's kingdom.

4. With thanksgiving, petition God for your daily needs. Tell Him about your desires. Ask Him to refine your desires to fit His. In Exodus 29:36–37, God gives instructions about the altar. He says that once the altar is purified with blood, "then the altar will be most holy, and whatever touches it will be holy." The true altar, of which the physical altar is a shadow, is within you. The true altar has been purified through the blood of Christ. Everything you place on His altar, He purifies and makes holy. Visualize yourself laying each desire on His altar.

Leave it there. He will work within you to purify your desires until they match His.

5. End your time with listening prayer. Commit yourself to listen for Him throughout the day. Ask Him to keep you in His presence.

6. You are not leaving Him now. You have fixed your mind on Him. You have nurtured your life for unceasing prayer.

Personal Prayer Retreats

You will find that as your hunger for God increases, your routine does not leave you enough time to spend alone with God. From time to time, God may call you out of your routine to give Him extended periods of time. You may feel the need for personal retreats.

A personal retreat may consist of a day, or a weekend, or a week. This will be a time when you are alone with God and uninterrupted. When I take a personal retreat, I take only my Bible and my journal. I don't take other books or tapes or work to do.

I have experimented with several settings for a personal retreat. I have tried having my husband and children gone while I stayed home. There were too many distractions for me to engage in extended prayer vigils. I tried going to a hotel. I found that if a television or telephone were available, I would "take a break" and soon find myself on another track. I have found a monastery where I can take a room for a day or a weekend. Here I have no distractions, and I am able to concentrate all my attention on God. You will have to find your own setting. You may not be as easily distracted as I am and may be able to have a personal retreat in your home.

God will train you in the way of prayer vigils. Your first personal retreat may be only a few hours. Don't be discouraged if you find your thoughts wandering, or if you don't live up to your own expectations. God will take responsibility for training you. If your thoughts wander, it may be the Holy Spirit directing them off your beaten path.

You are not expected to talk for hours during a prayer vigil. It will be primarily listening. Personal retreats are not necessarily somber occasions. For me, they are usually filled with great joy. Personal prayer retreats are often times filled with praise and worship. Let your thoughts wander. Turn all of your thoughts into prayers and let the Holy Spirit speak to you on the subjects of your thoughts. Have a long, rambling conversation with your dearest Friend.

You don't have to stay in one place during your retreat. Take a walk. Sit outside. This is not punishment. Enjoy the companionship of God. Take naps.

Prolonged Intercession

At times, God may call you to prolonged periods of intercession for a certain need. The burden of intercession will be strong and urgent. The Holy Spirit will allow you to identify strongly with the condition of the one for whom you are praying. Paul describes such a burden as being in labor. "My dear children, for whom I am again in the pains of childbirth until Christ is formed in you" (Galatians 4:19). The Holy Spirit will imprint His prayers on your heart, often through Scripture.

This call to prolonged, extraordinary intercession may be an indication that an intense spiritual battle is being waged. Your prayers are turning back the enemy, forcing him into retreat. The prophet Daniel had this experience.

Through the writings of Jeremiah, God burdened Daniel with the plight of his people. Daniel interceded earnestly according to the burden God had placed on him. While he was praying, Gabriel appeared to give him instruction about his intercession. Gabriel said, "'Daniel, I have now come to give you insight and understanding. As soon as you began to pray, an answer was given, which I have come to tell you, for you are highly esteemed'" (Daniel 9:22–23). Although Daniel labored in intercession for a prolonged time before he saw an answer, Gabriel said that the command had been issued at the beginning of his prayer. Daniel's prayers had mobilized spiritual forces and his persistence had defeated the enemy.

The tenth chapter of Daniel gives another vivid description of intercession. Daniel had been fasting and interceding for three weeks. When the answer to his intercession was delivered, the man in Daniel's vision said, "Do not be afraid, Daniel. Since the first day that you set your mind to gain understanding and to humble yourself before your God, your words were heard, and I have come in response to them. But the prince of the Persian kingdom resisted me twenty-one days. Then Michael, one of the chief princes, came to help me, because I was detained there with the king of Persia" (Daniel 10:12–13). Again, we get a glimpse into the spiritual battle raging beyond our physical senses. The first day that Daniel began to pray seeking understanding, his words were heard and the answer came in response to his words. It took 21 days of persevering prayer to overcome the unseen forces seeking to hinder God's answer.

It is important to respond to God's call to intercession. It is a privilege to give birth to God's plan by laboring in prayer.

Prayer and Fasting

God may call you to periods of prayer and fasting. Fasting is not a way to reach God. Fasting is not a way to get God's attention. Fasting is not a way to convince God that you're serious. Fasting does not work like a hunger strike; it will not back God into a corner and force Him to give in to your demands. Fasting is God's call to ignore the demands of your physical nature to respond to the demands of your spirit. For a short time, you may be called to abstain from physical nourishment and feast in your spirit. God wants to lead you into a form of prayer in which your spirit takes priority over your body in a tangible way. Jesus said, "'I have food to eat that you know nothing about. . . . My food is to do the will of him who sent me, and to finish his work'" (John 4:32, 34).

The purpose of fasting is not to get through to God, but to allow Him to get through to you. Jehoshaphat proclaimed a fast throughout Judah to seek God's word about how to deal with their enemies. His prayer was this: "'For we have no power to face this vast army that is attacking us. We do not know what to do, but our eyes are upon you'" (2 Chronicles 20:12). This should be the attitude of any fast. In disengaging ourselves from our physical world for a time, we fasten our attention on God.

During a fast, you should spend the time you would otherwise spend eating in prayer and seeking God. You might plan a fast during a personal retreat. Fasting is to be between you and God. Jesus warned His disciples not to fast to impress others. If you do, He warned, you will have settled for a short-term reward.

Do not fast if you have a medical condition that would make it harmful for you. Check with your doctor. You may want to start with a short fast. Forgo one meal and use that time in prayer and Bible study. You may need to engage in a modified fast. Drink fruit juices and clear broth.

Fasting is not a requirement. Don't let it become an obligation. God should initiate and maintain a fast. It will be a privilege and a joy. A time of fasting is a time of real intimacy. You will be a living sacrifice as you sacrifice meals to spend time in His presence.

Reasons for Fasting

A fast is for the Lord. "Ask all the people of the land and the priests, 'When you fasted and mourned . . . , was it really for me that you fasted?'" (Zechariah 7:5). Any spiritual discipline can become an empty form, a service or ritual. The Holy Spirit is the guard against legalism. He must appoint your fast. He must empower your fast and direct your fast.

In Isaiah 58, God reprimands His people for ceremonial fasting that excluded the spirit of the law. God said that all their rule-following, all their apparent righteousness, was useless because it did not change the way they conducted themselves. Even while they were fasting, they were oppressing others. The form means nothing to God unless it is an expression of an inner attitude. He would prefer that we skip the form if the spirit is not right. "'Oh, that one of you would shut the temple doors, so that you would not light useless fires on my altar! I am not pleased with you,' says the Lord Almighty, 'and I will accept no offering from your hands'" (Malachi 1:10).

When fasting is Spirit-led, it gives God access to you. It breaks down barriers that might have been erected. It increases your receptivity to Him. The result of fasting will show up in your living.

"'Is not this the kind of fasting I have chosen: to loose the chains of injustice and untie the cords of the yoke, to set the oppressed free and break every yoke? Is it not to share

your food with the hungry and to provide the poor wan-
derer with shelter—when you see the naked, to clothe him,
and not to turn away from your own flesh and blood?"
(Isaiah 58:6–7).

Meditation

How easily I trade away my eternal birthright for momentary ease.
I want quick fixes and easy answers. I will give You words of love,
but not my time. The disquiet in my soul never ends.

Everything you're searching for is waiting here, in Me.

"Come to me . . . I will give you rest" (Matthew 11:28).

Reflection

Schedule a few hours or a day for personal retreat. Take your Bible
and a journal. Use the time for fasting and prayer.

Review

1. Why is scheduled daily prayertime necessary?

2. What is the purpose of a fast?

3. How can spiritual disciplines become legalistic?

Teaching Guide

by Edna Martin Ellison

Introduction

This teaching guide gives plans for a two-hour session. Or you can adapt these ideas to a 12-week study.

The activities suggested may be used during a prayer retreat lasting more than two hours. If you chose to have a two-hour retreat, allow three hours so that you may give a break at midpoint.

Preplanning

Do the following things well in advance of the session(s):

1. Order adequate copies of *Heart's Cry*, allowing four to six weeks for delivery. Distribute these at least a week prior to the study, if possible.

2. Publicize the study, using announcements in worship services, organizational meetings, bulletins, and newsletters. Write cards to potential participants who might not otherwise hear of the study.

3. Read the entire book, making notes as you go. Complete the personal learning activities.

Study Planning

You know your participants better than anyone. Plan with specific people in mind. Think of the talents of your audience as you plan activities. Be prepared to deviate from this plan to fulfill the needs of your audience. Remember that adults vote with their feet. If they think this study will be boring, they simply will not come. Think of ways to incorporate fun into the learning experience.

Depending on the local situation, prepare these things:

1. Arrange the meeting room so that participants will sense a good learning atmosphere.

3. Remind participants to bring Bibles, *Heart's Cry,* paper, and pens.

4. Arrive early so you can greet each participant.

5. Plan to begin on time and end on time.

6. Pray for several weeks before the study begins. Ask others to pray with you about the success of this prayer retreat/study.

Items marked with three stars (***) require advance preparation.

Delight in the Lord
(Chapter 1)

***Duplicate the pretest "Prayer Life Evaluation" before the meeting.

Give out the pretest as participants enter.

Prayer Life Evaluation

(Check all that apply.)

1. My prayer life
   - ❏ a. is satisfactory
   - ❏ b. needs more time in my life
   - ❏ c. leads me to delight in God's Word daily
   - ❏ d. is totally fulfilling
   - ❏ e. needs strengthening

2. The following things interfere with my prayer life:
   - ❏ a. the cares of my workday
   - ❏ b. the cares of my home
   - ❏ c. other family members
   - ❏ d. personal problems
   - ❏ e. my time schedule

3. I hope to achieve the following things in this retreat/study:
   - ❏ a. an answer to problems in my life
   - ❏ b. knowledge of Scripture
   - ❏ c. steps to help me know how to pray
   - ❏ d. a fulfilling prayer life, pleasing to God
   - ❏ e. joy in prayer
   - ❏ f. fellowship with stronger Christians
   - ❏ g. a closer relationship with Jesus

Pray Without Ceasing
(Chapter 2)

***Prepare to lead a discussion in a large group, giving your opinion of: *Prayer is not an activity, but a relationship.*

A Clean Heart
(Chapter 3)

Make handouts of the examples and instructions below or write them on a chalkboard. Decide which activity your group would be comfortable using, or give them a choice.

Write a poem called "Refiner's Fire" on the topic of Christ's ability to purify your heart. The poem may be a couplet (two lines that rhyme), a sonnet (14 lines that can rhyme as follows: abab cdcd efef gg), or a haiku (Japanese poetry of 17 unrhymed syllables in 3 lines: 5 syllables in line 1, 7 syllables in line 2, and 5 syllables in line 3). You may also want to write a cinquain [sin-cain]:

Line 1: One noun (naming word)
Line 2: Two adjectives (words that describe the word in line 1)
Line 3: Three verbs (action words)
Line 4: A short phrase or sentence
Line 5: One noun (may be the same as line 1 or a similar word).

Finally, you may write free verse (unrhymed) or any assortment of poetic words of praise.

Examples:
1. Couplet
   Dear Lord, Your love is sure.
   O Christ, make my heart pure.

2. Sonnet
   For years I struggled with a heavy heart
   In sin and darkness, seldom to be free

From chains that bound me, kept me held apart
From light and truth and peace or eyes that see.

And deeper still I mired, though hard I tried
To surface upward to the truth and light;
Then in my misery and sin, I cried
"O God, I beg you to restore my sight!"

He heard, and in His mercy touched my soul;
He took my habits, filthy rags, and dirt.
With His refining fire He made me whole
And burned away my dark despair and hurt.

O Christ, You hurt on darkest Calvary.
Great Resurrection Light, Refining Fire. I'm free!

3. Haiku
   Savior of the world,
   Shed Your light upon us all
   Pure Refiner's Fire.

4. Cinquain
   Jesus
   Loving, Reaching
   Saves, Cleans, Redeems
   His Refiner's Fire purifies me.
   Christ

5. Free Verse
   Like a furnace power to refine,
   God's Holy Spirit
   tempers, cleans, and steels my heart
   to face tomorrow
   strong.

He Who Loves Me
(Chapter 4)

***Make a handout with the following principles listed on one side and the true-false quiz on the other side of the sheet.
***Lead in 1 and 2 below as small-group activities. Share answers.

1. Explain how these principles apply to your life:
   a. Obedience is the door to revelation.
   b. Obedience stems from a pure heart.
   c. Obedience grows from a personal relationship.
   d. Obedience brings freedom.
   e. Obedience increases your delight in the Lord.
   f. Obedience involves risk.

2. True or False:

____ 1. I do not have to be afraid to take my pain and anger to God.
____ 2. God may reject me if I admit I have an angry heart.
____ 3. God is not fragile. I can ask Him the hardest questions.
____ 4. God is calling me now to risk something.
____ 5. I am afraid to lay all on the altar.
____ 6. 1 am struggling with obedience.

Pray in the Spirit
(Chapter 5)

***Prepare envelopes for each participant (see *Heart's Cry,* p. 62). Designate a table as an altar to God. Early during the meeting ask participants to sign their names on blank strips of paper. While you are engaging in other activities (such as those suggested for chap. 4), ask someone to tape these strips on an 8½-by-11-inch sheet of paper, underneath the following words:

The child of God below is sealed in Christ, as a letter is sealed in an envelope. This person is stamped with God's personal seal and is truly one of His own. This person is safe, secure, and protected. The Holy

Spirit abides within; God is in control; Jesus is Savior. This person rests in perfect peace.

Instruct participants to do the following on the back of this sheet.

Dear Child of God,

Answer the questions in *Heart's Cry* on page 70. Write your feelings about each one. When you have completed the questions (a through e), commit yourself to walk in the Spirit as God leads you. Seal the envelope, and in an attitude of prayer, lay it on the altar.

In Everything Give Thanks
(Chapter 6)

Divide participants into small groups. Form circles of four to six people. Give these instructions: *Practice thanking God in short sentences. Take turns praying this sentence: Thank You, God, for_____ (one short phrase).* Continue around the circle for five to ten minutes.

Stand in the Gap
(Chapter 7)

Tell the story of the Coads on page 86. Ask participants to share similar experiences of intercessory prayer. Brainstorm ways to pray for missionaries.

Ask . . . Seek . . . Knock
(Chapter 8)

***1. Make a poster listing the three phrases below. Bring a large marker to fill in group responses.

ASK and keep on asking, and . . .

SEEK and keep on seeking, and . . .

KNOCK and keep on knocking, and . . .

Ask participants to finish each line of the acrostic aloud. Record answers on the poster. (Matthew 7:8–9)

2. Ask participants to list personal needs and present each one to God in prayer for His supply.

If Two Agree
(Chapter 9)

List steps for forming various kinds of prayer groups.

Upon This Rock
(Chapter 10)

*** Duplicate before the meeting:

Fill in the blank using ideas from *Heart's Cry*, chapter 10.

1. The church is the full expression of _____
2. The church is individuals _____
3. The church must be purified _____
4. The church has access to_____
5. God seeks churches who follow _____
6. God uses _____
7. God reveals Himself through the _____
8. Obedient churches usually _____

Words to choose:
    a. fused into one body
    b. by Refiner's Fire
    c. Him
    d. praying churches
    e. Christ
    f. Holy Spirit
    g. eternal resources
    h. engage in ministry

Answers: 1. e; 2. a; 3. b; 4. g; 5. c; 6. d; 7. f; 8. h

Be Still and Know
(Chapter 11)

*** 1. Set up equipment. Play several radios, televisions, or CD players at the same time. Turn the volume louder until someone complains. Then cut off all the "noisemakers." Explain that the world's noises can distract us from listening to the still, small voice of God.

2. Read Psalm 46:10; Psalm 31:20; Psalm 91:1; Psalm 25:14; and Proverbs 3:32. Then whisper the following sentences in someone's ear and ask her to pass the message until the last person in the room hears it. Whisper: *Members of Faith Baptist Church in Saskatchewan, Canada, committed themselves to seeking and following God. They were astounded at results. Students Gerry and Connie Taillon were saved and later became catalytic missionaries.*

Ask the last person to tell what she heard in the whisper. Compare her message to the one you began. Say: *As a church, we need to cooperate with each other as we listen to the still, small voice. This is a discipline; it does not happen naturally.*

Draw Aside
(Chapter 12)

Close with a prayer of commitment to put into practice ideas God has urged each participant to act upon. As an alternative, you may want to ask each participant to look at the pretest she took at the beginning of this retreat/study. Ask her to see how many of her expectations were reached during the meeting. Thank God for His leading.

Six years ago, God laid on my heart the need to pray for our children and their school. I learned about Moms in Touch and wanted to start a group.

The burden on my heart to begin the prayer group was so great that I finally chose a date and invited some friends for an introduction coffee. The date was Thursday, September 13, 2001. Little did I know why that was the date God had chosen. Due to the events of Tuesday, September 11, a large group of women gathered at my home to learn about praying in one accord for our children and schools and committed to meeting each week to cover our school in prayer.

When I was ready, God brought more women. We have been praying faithfully for that elementary school for many years.

Dana Grindal
Area Coordinator
Moms in Touch International

HOW TO KNOW GOD

Introduction

Have you ever stroked the velvety petal of a rose? Or listened to the restful cascade of a mountain stream? Or strolled in awe through a redwood grove? In these quiet moments, a thought may well up from your soul: *Only God could create such beauty.*

Most people who have experienced moments like these come away believing that there must be a God. But how does a person relate to this Creator? How do we come to know God?

The most marvelous book in the world, the Bible, marks the path to God with four vital truths. Let's look at each marker in detail.

Our Spiritual Condition: Totally Depraved?

The first truth is rather personal. One look in the mirror of Scripture, and our human condition becomes painfully clear:

As it is written,
"There is none righteous, not even one;
There is none who understands,
There is none who seeks for God;
All have turned aside, together they have become useless;
There is none who does good,
There is not even one." Romans 3:10–12

We are sinners through and through—totally depraved. Now that doesn't mean we've committed every atrocity known to humankind. We're not as *bad* as we can be, just as *bad off* as we can be. Sin colors all our thoughts, motives, words, and actions.

Don't believe it? Look around. Everything around us bears the smudge marks of our sinful nature. Despite our best efforts to create a perfect world, crime statistics continue to soar, divorce rates keep climbing, and families keep crumbling.

Something has gone terribly wrong in our society and in ourselves, something deadly. For, contrary to how the world would repackage it, "me first" living does not equal rugged individuality and freedom; it equals death. As Paul says in his letter to the Romans, "The wages of sin is death" (Romans 6:23)—our emotional and physical death through sin's destructiveness, and our spiritual death from God's righteous judgment of our sin.

This brings us to the second marker: God's character.

God's Character: Infinitely Holy

Our very awareness that things are not as they should be points to a standard of goodness beyond ourselves. That standard is God Himself. And God's standard of holiness contrasts starkly to our sinful condition.

Scripture says that "God is light, and in Him there is no darkness at all" (1 John 1:5). He is absolutely righteous—which creates a problem for us. If He is so pure, how can we who are so impure relate to Him?

Perhaps we could try being better people, try to tilt the balance in favor of our good deeds. Throughout history, people have attempted to live up to God's standard by keeping the Ten Commandments. Unfortunately, no one can come close to satisfying the demands of God's law. J. B. Phillips' translation of Romans 3 states:

No man can justify himself before God by a perfect performance of the Law's demands—indeed it is the straight-edge of the Law that shows us how crooked we are. Romans 3:20 Phillips

Our Need: A Substitute

So here we are, sinners by nature, sinners by choice, trying to pull ourselves up by our own bootstraps and attain a relationship with our holy Creator. But every time, we fall flat on our faces. We can't live a good enough life to make up for our sin, because God's standard isn't "good enough"—it's perfection. And we can't make amends for the offense our sin has created without dying for it. Who can get us out of this mess? If someone could live perfectly, honoring God's law, and would bear sin's death penalty for us, then we would be saved from our predicament. But is there such a person? Thankfully, yes!

Meet your substitute—*Jesus Christ*. He is the One who took death's place for you!

[God] made [Jesus Christ] who knew no sin to be sin on our behalf, that we might become the righteousness of God in Him.
2 Corinthians 5:21

God's Provision: A Savior

God rescued us by sending His Son, Jesus, to die for our sins on the cross (see 1 John 4:9–10). Jesus was fully human and fully divine, a truth that ensures His understanding of our weaknesses, His power to forgive, and His ability to bridge the gap between God and us (see Romans 5:6–11). In short, we are "justified as a gift by His grace through the redemption which is in Christ Jesus" (Romans 3:24). Two words in this verse bear further explanation: *justified* and *redemption*.

Justification is God's act of mercy, in which He declares believing sinners righteous, while they are still in their sinning state. Justification doesn't mean that God *makes* us righteous, so that we never sin again, rather He declares us righteous much like a judge pardons a guilty criminal. Because Jesus took our sin upon Himself and suffered our judgment on the cross, God forgives our debt and proclaims us PARDONED.

Redemption is God's act of paying the ransom price to release us from our bondage to sin. Held hostage by Satan, we were shackled by the iron chains of sin and death. Like any loving parent whose child has been kidnapped, God willingly paid the ransom. And what a price He paid! He gave His only Son to bear all the sins of humankind: past, present, and future. Jesus's death and resurrection broke our chains and set us free to become children of God (see Romans 6:16–18, 22; Galatians 4:4–7).

Placing Your Faith in Christ

These four truths describe how God has provided a way to Himself through Jesus Christ. But God won't force us to follow it. He won't drag us down a path we don't want to go. It's our decision to step forward into a relationship with Him, and we do so in faith.

For by grace you have been saved through faith; and that not of yourselves, it is the gift of God; not as a result of works, that no one should boast. Ephesians 2:8-9

We accept God's gift of salvation simply by placing our faith in Christ alone for the forgiveness of our sins. Would you like to enter a relationship with your Creator by trusting in Christ as your Savior? If so, here's a simple prayer you can use to express your faith:

Dear God,

I know that my sin has put a barrier between You and me. Thank You for sending Jesus to die in my place. I trust in Jesus alone to forgive my sins and accept His gift of eternal life. I ask Jesus to be my personal Savior and the Lord of my life. Thank You. In Jesus' name, amen.

If you prayed this prayer and want to know more about how to grow in this exciting new relationship, the first thing you need to do is tell someone about your decision. Do you know someone who is a born-again Christian? If not, is there a church in your neighborhood that you can call? You will find that getting connected with other believers is essential to maturing.

Second, let us know about your decision so we can help and encourage you in your new walk. Send in this form.

I have accepted Jesus Christ as my personal Lord and Savior. I would like to know more about how to follow Him.

Name _____

Address _____

Email address _____

Mail this form to:
The Praying Life Foundation
P. O. Box 1113
Blue Springs, MO 64013

Here are some Web sites where you will find resources and encouragement:

www.insight.org
www.nationaldayofprayer.org
www.prayinglife.org

When our children were young, we young mothers formed a babysitting co-op. At monthly meetings, we shared prayer requests (husband's job, child's ear infections, sleep, and so on). We decided to begin meeting weekly just for prayer. We had two rules: the hostess could not clean house before we arrived, and there would be no food. We met Monday nights at 9:00 *p.m.* after our little ones' bedtime while our husbands watched football, and we shared prayer requests, prayed, and resisted offering each other advice. We prayed as the Spirit led. That was in 1995. We still meet weekly, and it is the same four core members.

Our prayer partners are the first people we call when there is a need or a celebration. We've watched our children grow up and our husbands change jobs. And God has been right there with us through it all.

Pamm Coleman
Houston, Texas

Benefits of a Daily Relationship with Jesus Christ

By Jim Weidmann

The benefits of following Jesus are enormous. God wants each of us to experience these wonderful blessings, if only we will come to Him in reverent submission. Below are several reasons why we should be willing to seek a daily relationship with Christ.

1. A spiritual connection that will last forever.

God wants you to experience His joy on a regular basis in this life as well as throughout eternity. When you accepted Christ, you received spiritual vitality through your daily relationship with Him.

Psalm 16:11
Jeremiah 31:3
Matthew 25:46
John 3:14–16
John 3:36
John 4:13–14
John 5:24
John 6:39–40
John 10:27–28
John 17:1–3
Romans 5:21

Romans 6:22–23
2 Corinthians 4:17 to 5:1

2. Assurance of God's unconditional love.

Christ bridges the gap between you and God. Through a relationship with Jesus you are assured of His unconditional love for you. No matter what you have done or will do, since you have a relationship with Jesus, God will love you. He is always present and ready to help those who put their trust in Christ.

1 Timothy 1:14
John 3:16
John 16:27
Romans 5:8
Romans 8:35–39
Ephesians 2:4–5
Ephesians 3:17–19
1 John 3:1
1 John 4:7–10

3. Meaning and purpose in life.

Through a relationship with Christ, we realize that God is intimately aware of every aspect of our lives. We can trust that He will guide and direct us as we submit to Him and pray that He will lead us. Things may not always turn out as we would like them to, but we know that the Lord is in control and that His will is "perfect and pleasing" (Romans 12:2).

Furthermore, Christianity is grounded in historical and rational truth. As the apostle Paul put it, our faith is "true and reasonable." As such, it provides meaningful answers to the most difficult questions in life. This includes coherent moral foundation that clearly indicates right from wrong.

Acts 1:3
Acts 26:25
1 John 1:1–3

4. Strength to face each day.
Regardless of your circumstances, God will grant you strength when you seek His help. As you seek to serve the Lord, He will empower you to serve Him. Though difficulties will still arise, a firm foundation in Christ gives you the ability to face and overcome the challenges of life—everything from financial difficulties to dealing with family members and humanity in general.

Isaiah 41:10
John 16:33
Philippians 4:13
1 Timothy 1:12
2 Timothy 4:17

5. Peace.
God's peace does not exempt you from trials. Rather, it calms you and places your confidence in the Lord. As you experience difficulties and feel as though you are out of control, rest in the assurance that God is sovereign and always in control (Genesis 18:14).

Psalm 29:11
John 14:27
John 16:33
Acts 10:36
Romans 5:1
Ephesians 2:14–17
Philippians 4:6–7
Colossians 3:15

6. You become part of the body of Christ—the church.
When you receive Christ into your life, you become a part of a worldwide family of believers. Through participation in a local Christian church, believers are able to support one another on a regular basis.

Romans 12:4–5
1 Corinthians 12:13–14

Several years ago a friend asked me to join a prayer group with her and two other women. God urged me to go. I began to pray at that prayer group that God would lead me, guide me, and direct me in the way He would have me go. Then in 1997, I read an article about moms in Brazil who gathered to pray for their children involved in sexual immorality, drugs, and other concerns. That article would not leave my mind. After about a week, I went to see my pastor to ask him if we could simply have a day where the moms of our church would come and pray for their children. My pastor loved the idea and said, "Why don't we call it a Mom's Day of Prayer?" But as soon as I walked out of his office, I knew God was not calling me to do this just for my church but for the whole community—moms of all denominations, all races, all socioeconomic groups, and any women who wanted to pray for their children and the children of the world. That is how Mom's Day of Prayer (MDOP) started in January 1998. Now MDOP facilitates women all over the world to have Mom's Day of Prayer.

Kathy Coleman
President, Mom's Day of Prayer

RESOURCES FOR FURTHER STUDY

Chapter 1
More about the two covenants:
The Two Covenants by Andrew Murray
Our Covenant God by Kay Arthur

More about listening to God in His Word and meditating on Scripture:
Riches Stored in Secret Places by Jennifer Kennedy Dean
Simple Faith by Charles Swindoll

More about the tabernacle:
Restore My Heart by Denise Glenn
The Tabernacle by M. R. DeHaan
The Tabernacle: Shadows of the Messiah by David M. Levy
Man: God's Dwelling Place by A. W. Tozer
A Woman's Heart, God's Dwelling Place by Beth Moore

Chapter 2
More about unceasing prayer:
Live a Praying Life by Jennifer Kennedy Dean
PrayerStreaming by Janet Holm McHenry
Abide in Christ by Andrew Murray
Prayer by O. Hallesby

More about the blood of Christ:
The Life-Changing Power in the Blood of Christ by Jennifer Kennedy Dean

Chapter 3
More about a pure heart:
He Restores My Soul by Jennifer Kennedy Dean
Brokenness by Nancy Leigh Demoss

Chapter 4
More about obedience:
Fueled by Faith by Jennifer Kennedy Dean

Chapter 5
More about praying in the Spirit:
Live a Praying Life by Jennifer Kennedy Dean
The Healing Power of Prayer by Jennifer Kennedy Dean

Chapter 6
More about praise and thanksgiving:
31 Days of Praise by Ruth Meyer

Chapter 7
More about standing in the gap:
Live a Praying Life by Jennifer Kennedy Dean
Prayer by O. Hallesby
Every Child Needs a Praying Mom by Fern Nichols

Chapter 8
More about persevering prayer:
Live a Praying Life by Jennifer Kennedy Dean

Chapter 9
More about agreeing prayer:
What Happens When Women Pray by Evelyn Christenson

Chapter 10
More about the prayer power of the church:
Fresh Wind, Fresh Fire by Jim Cymbala
Fresh Encounter by Daniel Henderson
What the Spirit Is Saying to the Churches by Henry Blackaby

Chapter 11
More about listening prayer:
Riches Stored in Secret Places by Jennifer Kennedy Dean
He Leads Me Beside Still Waters by Jennifer Kennedy Dean

Chapter 12
More about drawing aside daily:
He Restores My Soul by Jennifer Kennedy Dean
He Leads Me Beside Still Waters by Jennifer Kennedy Dean
Certain Hope in Uncertain Times by Shirley Dobson

More General Prayer Resources
PrayerWalking by Janet Holm McHenry
Every Child Needs a Praying Mom by Fern Nichols
The Life-Changing Power in the Name of Jesus by Jennifer Kennedy Dean
Becoming a Woman of Prayer by Cynthia Heald
Legacy of Prayer by Jennifer Kennedy Dean

Web Sites
www.nationaldayofprayer.org
www.prayinglife.org
www.momsintouch.org

I often tell moms that in our world we will be tempted by busyness and activities on behalf of our children, but the very best thing we can do is pray and pray together. I have seen the results of sustaining prayer for our kids and their schools as well as ourselves. The sense of connection and the power of connected prayer always amaze me.

Cindy Bledsoe
Falls Church, Virginia

Prayer FAQs

By Jennifer Kennedy Dean

Why do we pray? What does prayer do?
God has set up the cosmos (the created order, including both heaven and earth) so that prayer is the conduit through which His intervening power and His provision flow from heaven to the circumstances of earth. He has chosen to engage His people in everything He wants to do on the earth, first through prayer, then through obedience. Prayer activates the specific will of God in earth's circumstances. Jesus prayed, "Let Your will be done in this circumstance on earth in the same way that Your will is in effect in heaven." (My interpretation of Matthew 6:10).
See chapter 7.

How can I know God's will?
When you enter into a relationship with God through Jesus Christ, God's Spirit has access to your mind and heart. He can speak to you, and He knows the mind and the will of God. Paul, speaking of those things that we can't know by our physical sense or by human knowledge, says, "God has revealed it to us by his Spirit. The Spirit searches all things, even the deep things of God" (1 Corinthians 2:10).

God uses Scripture to reveal His will to you. He speaks the truth of His Word to you by His Holy Spirit and causes His Word to live—take up residence—in you, progressively transforming your thoughts so that they come to echo His. "If you remain in me and my words remain in you, ask whatever you wish, and it will be given you" (John 15:7–8).
See chapter 5.

Isn't God going to do His will anyway?

To me, the most amazing thing about prayer is that God has ordained it for His purposes and has established it to be the conductor of His power and provision. In the Big Picture, nothing that God plans will be thwarted. His purposes stand firm through all generations. Yet, He makes it clear in His Word that "you do not have, because you do not ask God" (James 4:2). He is never without faithful intercessors somewhere whose prayers are the circuits conducting His provision and plan into the earth. On the other hand, there is power and provision available for every detail of your life that is left untapped because of lack of prayer.

See chapter 7.

How much of God's will can I know? For what purpose does God reveal some element of His will to me?

God reveals to you that which you need to know to pray effectively and to live in obedience. He does not become your personal fortune-teller. He does not speak to satisfy your curiosity. He speaks to author prayer and to awaken faith.

See chapter 11.

What about when God doesn't answer my prayers?

God never withholds good from you. Sometimes we think we know best what God should do and how He should answer our prayers, but true faith in God rests on our confidence in God's wisdom and love. Often, when you think that God has not answered your prayers, the truth is that He is answering your heart's cry.

If you find that you rarely experience answers to prayer, then consider whether God is speaking to you about sin and disobedience in your life that is clogging up the flow of His provision and diminishing your ability to hear Him.

See chapters 1, 3, and 4.

What difference does my obedience and purity make in the power of my prayers?

Since prayer is a conduit through which God's power flows, if that conduit is clogged, then the power flow is diminished or even blocked.

See chapters 3 and 4.

Is it selfish to pray for things for myself?
God invites us to ask Him for everything we need, big or little.

Why do we ask other people to pray for us?
Scripture makes it clear that there is multiplied power in multiplied prayer. Deuteronomy 32:30 says that one can chase 1,000, but two can put 10,000 to flight. Multiplied power.
See chapters 9 and 10.

Why do we pray in groups?
God wants His people to live in unity, so He has set up the dynamics of prayer to accomplish that end. "I tell you that if two of you on earth agree about anything you ask for, it will be done for you by my Father in heaven. For where two or three come together in my name, there am I with them" (Matthew 18:19–20). In the context of group prayer, the Holy Spirit can reveal and teach through the group. We feed each other's faith and stand firm when another is faltering.
See chapters 9 and 10.

Why do I need to be part of a body of believers?
God does not intend that an individual believer's prayer life will reach its full potential outside the context of the church.
See chapter 10

When should I pray? How long should I pray?
The discipline of prayer should not become a legalism. There is no set time or no prescribed length of time. Most people who take prayer seriously find that early morning is the best time to be alone for an extended period. The main thing is to find a time daily that works for you and stick to it.
See chapter 12.

*New Hope® Publishers is a division of WMU®,
an international organization that challenges Christian believers
to understand and be radically involved in God's mission.
For more information about WMU, go to www.wmu.com.
More information about New Hope books may be found
at www.newhopepublishers.com. New Hope books
may be purchased at your local bookstore.*